THUNDER OVER THE PRAIRIE

THUNDER
OVER THE PRAIRIE

THE TRUE STORY OF A MURDER AND A MANHUNT BY THE GREATEST POSSE OF ALL TIME

HOWARD KAZANJIAN
AND CHRIS ENSS

TWODOT®

GUILFORD, CONNECTICUT
HELENA, MONTANA
AN IMPRINT OF THE GLOBE PEQUOT PRESS

To buy books in quantity for corporate use
or incentives, call **(800) 962–0973**
or e-mail **premiums@GlobePequot.com.**

A · **T W O D O T**® · **B O O K**

Text design: Sheryl P. Kober
Project manager: Julie Marsh
Layout: Joanna Beyer
Map: M.A. Dubé and Jeff Galpin © Morris Book Publishing, LLC

Library of Congress Cataloging-in-Publication data is available.

ISBN 978-0-7627-4493-0

Printed in the United States of America

10 9 8 7 6 5 4 3 2

FOR DORA

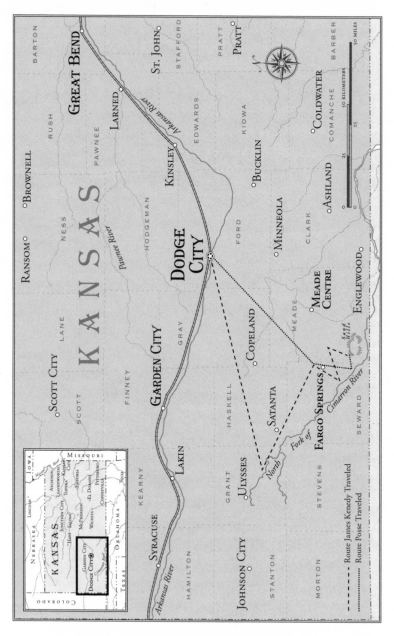

*This 1908 map of Kansas shows the routes traveled by the
"intrepid posse" and gunman James Kenedy.*

Based on information provided by Kansas Heritage Center, Dodge City

CONTENTS

FOREWORD

D odge City, Kansas, founded in 1872, when the Atchison, Topeka, and Santa Fe Railroad reached a point five miles west of Fort Dodge, was a wide-open, raucous frontier town that at first catered to buffalo hunters—from 1872 through 1875. Following the demise of the buffalo trade, the City Fathers went south to entice Texas ranchers to bring their longhorn cattle to Dodge City where they would receive top prices for their beef. It was during this period, from 1875 until 1885, that Dodge City enjoyed the dubious distinction of being the "Queen of the Cowtowns."

During this reign Dodge City, also known as the "wickedest little city in America," was the scene of many famous and some infamous incidents that would forever pique the interest of writers and create the lasting legends of some of the real people who resided here. The year 1878 provided all of the right stuff that would put Dodge City on the map as a wild-and-wooly cow town and helped establish its permanent place in the annals of those bygone days.

It was during that year that four young and fearless men (among others) in their twenties and early thirties, Wyatt Earp, Bat Masterson, Bill Tilghman, and Charlie Bassett, were hired to uphold the law; James "Dog" Kelley was elected mayor; Marshal Ed Masterson, Bat's brother, was shot and killed in the line of duty by an unruly cowboy; J. H. "Doc" Holiday, dentist, office in room 24 of the Dodge House, offered his services with "money refunded if not satisfied, " his ad promised; Assistant U.S. Deputy Marshal Henry T.

McCarty was shot and killed in the Long Branch Saloon; Dull Knife and his band of 340 Cheyenne jumped the reservation at Fort Reno and fled north through western Kansas to their North Dakota homeland; Col. William H. Lewis, commander at Fort Dodge, was killed in a battle while pursuing the Cheyenne in northwestern Kansas; and a beautiful singer-entertainer, Dora Hand was foully murdered by a young cattle baron who was smitten by her charms.

This book, *Thunder Over the Prairie,* by Howard Kazanjian and Chris Enss, does a masterful job relating the murder of Dora Hand and the subsequent pursuit and capture of her killer by those four young lawmen. The authors convincingly present these men as real people who were very good at doing their job, not just the mythical icons of the "Old West" that they would later become.

A local historian, Fredric R. Young, in his book, *Dodge City: Up Through a Century in Story and Pictures,* states, "Much nonsense has been written about Dodge City's Queen of the Fairy Belles, Dora Hand, but her romantic and novel history is yet to be fully unraveled."

It is my humble opinion that 140 years after her death, this gripping and suspenseful book is a beautiful unraveling of her romantic and novel history.

— JIM SHERER, DIRECTOR (RETIRED)
OF KANSAS HERITAGE CENTER AND
FORMER MAYOR OF DODGE CITY, KANSAS

ACKNOWLEDGMENTS

It would have been impossible to create this book without the cooperation of persons and institutions that provided the historical information. We are deeply indebted to the following organizations and individuals for their generous assistance.

The New England Historical Genealogical Research Department for the background material supplied on Dora Hand. The report was concise, thorough, and enlightening.

Elaine Grublin, assistant librarian at the Massachusetts Historical Society.

The National Archives Department in Washington, D.C., the Library of Congress, the American Museum of Natural History in New York, the California State Library, and the Denver Public Library, Western History Department.

Michael Church, the manuscripts archivist at the Kansas State Historical Society. He was obliging and patient.

The staff at the Fort Dodge Museum and the Kansas Heritage Center, in particular its director, Jim Sherer. We are indebted to the kindness of Mr. Sherer and the other historians for their expertise and attention to detail.

Our deepest thanks extend to Erin Turner at The Globe Pequot Press for her faith in this project and dedication to the process.

INTRODUCTION

O n their way to becoming legends of the Old West, Sheriffs Charlie Bassett and Bat Masterson and Deputies Wyatt Earp and Bill Tilghman patrolled the unruly streets of Dodge City, Kansas. All four of the men were police officers who held varying titles while working for two different entities, which they could do at the same time. Sheriffs and their deputies were elected by voters and were paid employees of the city. Marshalls and their deputies were appointed by a public official and paid by the federal government. The four lawmen endeavored to keep the peace between rowdy cowhands fresh off the trail and the local citizens who wanted to transform the "wickedest little city in America" into a civilized community. Many cowboys resisted law and order and dared the police to stop them from shooting up the town, robbing strangers, and gunning people down in the streets.

Often times the lawmen apprehended and arrested a felon at the scene of the crime, but occasionally the outlaw fled and the authorities would then recruit a group of men to go after them. Posses (the word *posse* is derived from the Latin term *posse comitatus,* which means "power of the county") were commonplace.

Forming a posse was one of the first actions taken whenever a desperado escaped from jail. The violators of the law were vigorously pursued and once captured were brought back to the place where they would stand trial. What made the posse that rode out of Dodge in October 1878 unique was the caliber of the police officers who participated in the search.

Wyatt, Bat, Charlie, and Bill were all experts with a gun and knew the surrounding terrain very well. They were part diplomats, part renegades, and all courage. Their hunt across the plains of Kansas for a cattle baron suspected of shooting a saloon singer named Dora Hand, strongly influenced their friendships, careers, and attitudes about the justice system.

More than two years of research has gone into the telling of the posse's ride. Numerous primary sources were used including the *Dodge City Times* and *Ford County Globe* newspapers, and the *Farmer's Almanack,* all dating from 1877 to 1881. Questions have been raised over the recent years as to the accuracy of the newspaper accounts about the posse. Some historians have suggested the reports were altered to show the ways in which police persecuted Texas cowhands who brought a generous portion of revenue into Dodge City. Others believe all the accounts, no matter how biased, have merit and stand as the most reliable source available about the killing of Dora Hand.

All of the sources consulted list the primary members of the posse as Wyatt Earp, Bat Masterson, Charlie Bassett, and Bill Tilghman. Deputies Neal Brown and William Duffy are mentioned as members of the posse, but with no consistency. Sometimes Neal Brown is mentioned as participating in the ride; other times William Duffy's name is noted, and then there are accounts that do not mention either of the men at all. For that reason we decided to focus on the lawmen referred to most often as being members of the posse. (The spelling of the names of the story participants is consistent with that in the majority of newspapers that covered the events.)

There are other components of this story that are difficult to verify, especially when firsthand accounts contradict one another. Many of these questionable details are noted in the text, but to list them all would lessen the impact of the story.

The purpose of this book is to tell the tale as an adventure and as a pivotal experience in the lives of these legendary lawmen. For more information about Dodge City or members of the posse consider *Dodge City: Up Through a Century in Story and Pictures* by Frederic R. Young, *Wyatt Earp: The Life Behind the Legend* by Casey Tefertiller, and *Bat Masterson: The Man and the Legend* by Robert K. DeArment.

Dora Hand's murder was one of the first ride-by shootings documented. The vicious crime and the story of men who went after the assassin make up an important chapter in not only the history of Dodge City, but of the Wild West.

CHAPTER ONE

MURDER OF A NIGHTINGALE

*Some of the proprieties were carefully observed . . . ,
for example, a woman, no matter whether she was a
housewife, a dance hall girl or even a courtesan (and
mind you, the last two were not necessarily the same),
was treated with grave courtesy on the street. Any man
who failed to observe this canon got into trouble.*

ACTOR EDDIE FOY CONCERNING
THE LADIES IN DODGE CITY, KANSAS, 1913

Dora Hand was in a deep sleep. Her bare legs were draped across the thick blankets covering her delicate form and a mass of long, auburn hair stretched over the pillow under her head and dangled off the top of a flimsy mattress. Her breathing was slow and effortless. A framed, graphite-charcoal portrait of an elderly couple hung above the bed on faded, satin-ribbon wallpaper and kept company with her slumber.

The air outside the window was still and cold. The distant sound of voices, backslapping laughter, profanity, and a piano's tinny, repetitive melody wafted down Dodge City's main thoroughfare and snuck into the small room where Dora was sleeping.

Dodge was an all-night town. Walkers and loungers kept the streets and saloons busy. Residents learned to sleep

1

through the giggling, growling, and gunplay of the cowboy consumers and their paramours for hire. Dora was accustomed to the nightly frivolity and clatter. Her dreams were seldom disturbed by the commotion.

All at once the hard thud of a pair of bullets charging through the door and wall of the tiny room cut through the routine noises of the cattle town with uneven, gusty violence. The first bullet was halted by the dense plaster partition leading into the bed chambers. The second struck Dora on the right side under her arm.[1] There was no time for her to object to the injury, no moment for her to cry out or recoil in pain. The slug killed her instantly.

In the near distance a horse squealed and its galloping hooves echoed off the dusty street and faded away.

A pool of blood poured out of Dora's fatal wound, turning the white sheets she rested on to crimson. A clock sitting on a nightstand next to the lifeless body ticked on steadily and mercilessly. It was 4:30 in the morning on October 4, 1878, and for the moment nothing but the persistent moonlight filtering into the scene through a closed window marked the thirty-four-year-old woman's passing.

Twenty-four hours prior to Dora's being gunned down in her sleep, she had been on stage at the Alhambra Saloon and Gambling House. She was a stunning woman whose wholesome voice and exquisite features had charmed audiences from Abilene to Austin. She regaled love-starved wranglers and rough riders at stage and railroad stops with her heartfelt rendition of the popular ballads "Blessed Be the Ties That Bind" and "Because I Love You So."

Adoring fans referred to her as the "nightingale of the frontier" and admirers continually competed for her attention. More times than not pistols were used to settle arguments about who would be escorting Dora back to her place at the end of the evening. Local newspapers claimed her talent and beauty "caused more gunfights than any other woman in all the West."[2]

The gifted entertainer was born Isadore Addie May on August 23, 1844, in Lowell, Massachusetts. At an early age she showed signs of being a more than capable vocalist, prompting her parents to enroll her at the Boston Conservatory of Music. Impressed with her ability, instructors at the school helped the young ingenue complete her education at an academy in Germany. From there she made her stage debut as a member of a company of operatic singers touring Europe.

After a brief time abroad, Dora returned to America. By the age of twenty-four she had developed a fondness for the vagabond lifestyle of an entertainer and was not satisfied being at any one location for very long. The need for musical acts beyond the Mississippi River urged her west and appreciative show-goers enticed her to remain there.[3]

In 1868 the theater troupe she was a part of was scheduled to appear on a handful of stages in the fastest growing railroad towns outside of Independence, Missouri. The first stop was Kansas City, Kansas. Settlers, trail hands, and ranchers were enchanted by Dora. She was showered with applause and praise and sought after by eligible bachelors both young and old. Enamored suitors insisted they would "wade through hell for one of her smiles."[4]

Capt. Theodore Hand, an attractive, athletically built cavalryman in his mid-thirties, was one such suitor. He called on Dora at the conclusion of one of her performances and something in his manner so appealed to her that she agreed to see him regularly. Theodore and Dora's relationship quickly grew from infatuation to love. A proposal of marriage followed a confession of their mutual feelings.[5]

Although she adored performing, Dora left the theater to become an army wife. She and Theodore moved to Fort Hays, Kansas, and were wed in the spring of 1871. Fort Hays was initially established to protect stages and freight wagons from attacks by Cheyenne and Arapaho Indians. It was also a supply depot for other forts in the area. Captain Hand accompanied regiments traveling back and forth with provisions for soldiers and their families stationed south and west of Fort Hays. Consequently, Dora was regularly left alone. The captain's infidelity and gambling habit made the long periods of separation unbearable. The Hands quarreled over Theodore's roving eye and his inability to keep and manage their limited finances. After several ultimatums were made and subsequently defied, Dora decided to leave her husband and return to a way of life she knew to be dependable, the theater, according to the September 24, 1878, edition of the *Ford County Globe*.

In an attempt to further distance herself from her estranged spouse, Dora changed her name to Fannie Keenan and made her way to St. Louis, where she found work singing and acting in the finest dance halls in the city. The gifted artist was just as well received by audiences then as she had been before her brief departure from the business. Critics said she brought "a sense of glamour and refinement" to the sometimes rustic venues where she performed.[6]

Men were enraptured by her voice and moved by the kindness she showed those who made a point of telling her how her smile and singing had won their hearts. By 1876 the itinerant entertainer had drifted into Texas, bewitching audiences across the Panhandle. An ambitious theatrical agent passing through the territory signed her to a performance troupe set to appear in the cattle communities of Abilene and Dodge City, Kansas. Both locations were "end of trail" towns for cowboys driving livestock north from San Antonio and points in between. Due in large part to its growing intolerance of the rowdy trail hands and its desire to become a respectable hamlet, Abilene had fewer overnight visitors than did Dodge City. As such, entertainers and their representatives preferred performing in the latter town, referred to by some as the "Queen of the Cowtowns."

A hot wind ushered Dora into Dodge in June of 1878. The sun's rays were like the flames of a furnace blasting down on the parched path leading into the city. Dust rose with each turn of the wheels of the stage she was aboard and sand swirled about the vehicle obscuring any view. Several of the city's residents were eagerly anticipating Hand's arrival. Among them was the mayor of Dodge City, James Kelley. Mayor Kelley had made Dora's acquaintance at Camp Supply in Oklahoma.[7]

Like everyone else who had the privilege of hearing her sing, he was inspired by her voice and intoxicated by her beauty. After becoming the proprietor of a local dance hall, he began soliciting her to perform there. Dora accepted his invitation, agreeing to appear at his establishment provided she would be permitted to entertain at other resorts in town.

The performer arrived in Dodge City with her housekeeper and a good friend, well-known entertainer Fannie Garrettson. When the three disembarked from the stage, they found the cow town a dizzying array of activity. Hack drivers spurred their vehicles up and down the street at a rapid pace, unconcerned with the pedestrians who were forced to jump out of their way. Harlots stood outside the doorways of their closet-sized dens, inviting passersby to step inside. Stray dogs wandered about barking and scrounging for food. Ranch hands led their bawling livestock into corrals or railroad cars. Disorderly drifters made their way to lively saloons, firing their pistols in the air as they went.

Dodge City, Kansas, was a community rooted in a military post. Fort Dodge, an army camp five miles from Dodge City, was established in 1865 to protect wagon trains from warring Plains Indians and to furnish supplies to soldiers fighting the Native Americans. The town, which was named after the fort, was founded in 1872 and quickly became a trade center for travelers and buffalo hunters. Its popularity increased with the coming of the railroad. Texas cattlemen drove their tremendous herds into the thriving burg and loaded the animals onto the Atchison, Topeka, and Santa Fe rail lines heading east.

The numerous, and often times wild, residents who populated Dodge were from all walks of life. Ambitious businessmen, Indian scouts, soldiers, homesteaders, Chinese railroad workers, gamblers, and soiled doves added to the character of the whistle-stop. An eclectic array of nocturnal entertainment was always available to hardworking pleasure seekers in Dodge. Whether it was attending bull-fights, visiting brothels owned by such renowned madams as Squirrel Tooth Alice, or taking in a show at one of many variety theaters, there was something for everyone.

In Dodge City's early days, law and order was more an abstract notion than a reality and it was seldom, if ever, enforced. Fights broke out and guns were pulled at the slightest provocation. For a short time a man could do as he pleased without fear of legal reprisals. Between the summers of 1872 and 1873, twenty-five people were shot and killed in Dodge and almost twice as many had been wounded in saloon brawls and gunfights. An East Coast newspaper proclaimed the town to be as "rough a community as ever flourished under one flag."[8]

Part of the reason for the town's riotous reputation is that the majority of the businesses at the whistle-stop catered to the rowdy trail hands. The financial growth of Dodge City depended in large part on the cowboys and their immoral conduct. The so-called respectable citizens of Ford County resented the violence and disorder but were willing to subject themselves to the unrestrained actions of these men for the sake of the fortunes to be made. Law enforcement officials were encouraged to overlook all but the most dangerous men and to essentially keep a lid on only the most violent crimes. Mercantile owners, restaurant operators, proprietors of saddle and boot shops, saloon keepers, and gambling hall managers feared that if the atmosphere became too strict, the ranch hands would take their business and money to a more hospitable town. In an effort to maintain a sense of order, the sheriff and his deputies had to be part politician and part lawman.

Shortly after Dora and Fannie arrived at their raucous destination, they walked down the city's main artery, known as Front Street, to the theater district. The pair had an engagement to play at the Comique Theatre. The women were signed to perform with a cast of entertainers that included can-can dancers, jugglers, cloggers, and magicians. Variety shows at the Comique went on all night, one act following another in rapid succession. Restless audiences weren't always quiet and attentive each time another performer took to the stage, however. Many times drunk and impatient patrons shouted over the entertainers and even shot at them if they were dissatisfied with the performance. The decorative setting in front of which the players performed was filled with several bullet holes, as was the ceiling above their heads.

The Comique Theatre had the least number of incidents of violence against performers of all the theaters in Dodge City. That was due in large part to the caliber of entertainers that appeared there. According to the July 30, 1878, edition of the *Ford County Globe*, the Comique was the "favorite place of resort—offering its patrons the best show or entertainment ever given in Dodge." Among the outstanding acts the paper listed as appearing at the theater were "ballad and variety performers Fannie Garrettson and Fannie Keenan" (better known as Dora Hand), "transformation dancer M'lle Cerito, and the musical comedy team of Foy and Thompson." The article also added that "all the members of this troupe are up in their parts and considerably above the average ability."

Dora followed her run at the Comique Theatre with a two-week benefit at Ham Bell's Varieties. Bell, who knew the songstress used both the name of Dora Hand and Fannie Keenan on stage, asked her how she wanted her name listed for the playbill. "What is your real name?" he inquired. "Well, Mister Bell," she said, "take your pick, one's just as good as the other." The August 10, 1878, edition of the *Dodge City Times* listed Dora Hand as one of the performers set to appear on stage along with celebrated actress Hattie Smith. The *Times* noted that the two women were "general favorites in Dodge and were sure to play to a full house."

During the day Dora served the community by helping to take care of the homeless and sick. Her benevolence sometimes extended to cowboys who had lost everything at the faro or poker tables. More than once she grubstaked a destitute trail hand's way home and out of debt. At night the dance hall singer thrilled audiences over and over again at a variety of venues. Engagements outside of town periodically took Dora away from the area for short periods of time, but the adoration of loyal bullwhackers and cowpunchers kept her coming back to the rough-and-tumble burg.

On September 24, 1878, after more than six years' separation from Theodore Hand, Dora filed for divorce. The Ford County, Kansas, petition read that "during the marriage and even since she has conducted herself as a true and faithful wife, fulfilling and performing all her duties as per the marriage contract." The decree claimed that Captain Hand had "deserted and abandoned Dora for Gizzie Gataun, a woman residing in Cincinnati, Ohio."[9]

News of the impending dissolution of Dora's marriage filled the hearts of would-be suitors with hope. James Kenedy, the handsome, overly indulged son of Texas cattle baron Mifflin Kenedy, was arrogant enough to believe he could make Dora his own. He had never met her, but rumors that circulated about her kindness and charm had captured his fancy and he was determined to sweep her off her feet.

James Kenedy was a tall man with a strong build and he was accustomed to getting his own way. He wore tailor-made clothes and carried himself with confidence derived mostly from his family's sizeable bank account and land holdings. When James strutted into the Alhambra Saloon and Gambling House in September 1878, it was with the intention of introducing himself to Dora, marrying her, and escorting her back to his ranch.

A mesmerized crowd surrounded the stage where she stood serenading them with a touching tune. Lost in delivering a moving performance, she barely noticed James pushing his way through the audience to find a seat near the front. Grateful regulars rose to their feet at the end of her song. James followed suit.[10]

Dora graciously took a bow and surrendered the stage to Fannie Garrettson. A bartender served Dora a cold drink as she settled herself at a table alone in the back of the room. While she was listening to the music, James strolled over to her and without invitation pulled up a chair and sat down. He placed a bottle of whisky and two glasses in front of her. His aggressive stance was met with polite indifference, and in spite of his attempts to engage her in conversation, Dora kept her focus on Fannie's performance.

"My name is James Kenedy," the persistent man offered as he poured himself a drink. "My friends call me Spike." "I know who you are, Mister Kenedy," Dora responded coolly. A broad smile filled his face as he studied her hair, her face, her clothes, the way she held her hands. She didn't dignify his boorish behavior with so much as a glance. Preoccupied with Dora's delicate features, James did not see Mayor James Kelley walk up behind them and place his hand lovingly on the songstress's shoulder.

Kelley was a formidable man in his mid-forties with a thick, droopy mustache and sparse, unkempt hair of indeterminate color. He was a former army scout who had worked with George Custer while they were stationed at Fort Dodge. When Custer left the area in 1872, he gave Mayor Kelley a number of his hunting dogs. The animals seldom if ever left Kelley's side. His entourage of prized greyhounds had earned him the nickname "Dog."

James and the mayor eyed one another carefully. Dora ever so slightly shifted her body toward Kelley and he smiled a satisfied smile. James's expression was grim. His history with the mayor was troubled. His family had sold Kelley a stolen horse some months back and news of the sale had besmirched the Kenedy name. James was certain Kelley had told Dora that the Kenedys were a family not to be associated with and that that was the reason she was ignoring him.

James had doubled his alcohol intake and was feeling no pain when he started cursing his rival. The whiskey made him bold and loud. He accused Kelley of ruining his chance to woo Dora. He vowed to have her regardless of what she or anyone else thought. Assuming some of James's riding buddies would escort their friend out of the saloon once his behavior became too obnoxious, Mayor Kelley tolerated the cowhand. When it was clear James would not be leaving, either on his own steam or with the help of his associates, Kelley jerked the man out of his seat and tossed him out of the tavern.[11]

Once James sobered up, the memory of the humiliating events sparked his desire for revenge. Armed with dangerously wounded pride, a .45-caliber pistol, and the financial backing that would deliver him from any illegal act, James vowed that Kelley would pay for his offenses.

The following morning a relentless sun peered through a partly cloudy sky and revealed the carnage left by wild Dodge City inhabitants like James who had been celebrating the previous evening. Broken glass, beer bottles, human waste, and the occasional drunken cowboy lay in the streets and alleyways. The smell of cattle, gunpowder, straw, manure, and cheap perfume mixed with the scent of fresh baked bread from the bakeries and ham and eggs from the various eateries on either side of the railroad tracks that ran down the center of town. Dora maneuvered around the hurried and aromatic scene, chaperoned by the mayor, her hand tucked in the crook of his arm.

James stood outside one of the town's numerous hotels, watching the pair interact. He was hung over and seething with anger. Disgusted and dejected, he turned away from the couple and took off in the opposite direction. Several loyal hands from his father's ranch followed after him.[12]

Dora and Mayor Kelley eventually concluded their outing and went their separate ways. The pack of dogs at Kelley's heels happily paraded behind him as he walked toward his home, situated behind the Great Western Hotel. Once inside the modest house, the mayor eased his frame into his comfortable bed in the front bedroom and attempted to take a nap. After a few moments he was roused out of his thin sleep by a noise in his yard. He listened, braced on one elbow. Glancing out the window and over the tops of the cannas and yucca plants that surrounded his residence, he spotted James coming up the gravel path leading to his front door.[13]

Mayor Kelley jumped out of bed and grabbed his six-shooter from a nearby nightstand. When he heard James's boots on the porch, he flung the door open and raised his gun level with the cattleman's chest. James was taken aback and for a quick second the two men stood staring at each other. Kelley was ready to fire if forced and James, backed up by a handful of armed men, was ready to draw if the mood and nerve struck him.

Tense silence gave way to a barrage of profanity. The pair exchanged insults and threats. Kelley ordered James off his property, and persuaded by his hired hands, the hot-headed cattleman eventually gave in. He backed up along the walkway, surveying Kelley's place as he went. His face was savage with the violent thoughts that he would act on later. Before he turned to leave, the wind stirred the curtains on the window in the front bedroom, and he caught a glimpse of the mayor's unmade bed. He paused for a moment to think, then grinned tolerantly at Kelley as he left.

On October 3, 1878, Dora Hand entertained another standing room only crowd at the Alhambra Saloon and Gambling House. She courteously accepted the enthusiastic applause, thanked the piano player for accompanying her, said goodnight to the audience, and exited the tavern to retire for the evening. Men milling around the streets playfully whistled and called after her as she walked by them. She hurried along undisturbed to Mayor Kelley's and entered the home as though she were expected.

Mayor Kelley was out of town and had invited Dora and her friend Fannie to stay at his place during his absence. The accommodations were infinitely more quiet and private than a hotel's. The performer tiptoed through the house making sure not to wake Fannie. After slipping into her bed clothes, she crawled under the covers and drifted off to sleep.[14]

The shots that pierced the walls of Kelley's home at 4:15 in the morning rousted Fannie Garrettson from her bed shortly after she'd heard them fired. An eerie stillness hung in the air—a quiet that begged her not to trust it. Fannie glanced down at the quilt across the bed and noticed a burn hole in the fabric. She knew it had been made by a bullet. Slipping her finger into the frayed material, she traced the path of the pistol ball to the wall opposite the bed.

Fannie raced out of the house, her eyes wide with terror, screaming. Shaking and hysterical, she sat down in the alleyway between Mayor Kelley's home and a row of saloons that bordered the building in the back. When the law arrived moments later to investigate, they found Fannie Garrettson in her nightgown sobbing and rocking back and forth. Too upset to speak, she merely pointed at the house and shook her head. "Poor Dora," she later told authorities, "she never spoke but died unconscious. She was so when she was struck and so she died."

CHAPTER TWO

COLD-BLOODED ASSASSIN

Any one gets it but the one for whom it is intended,
and particularly in this wretched city.

FANNIE GARRETTSON WRITING FROM
DODGE CITY, OCTOBER 5, 1878

A steady beat of boots hurrying along the wooden plank sidewalks reverberated off the buildings and overhangs lining Dodge City's Front Street. Curious onlookers peered out of the saloons and bathhouses as two familiar characters sprinted past. Lawmen Wyatt Earp and Jim Masterson, Bat Masterson's younger brother, raced in the direction of town from which a series of gunshots had popped five minutes earlier.[1]

Both men wore the stern, focused look of peace officers accustomed to living in a dangerous and unpredictable cow town. Each had a commanding presence that warded off as many as it attracted. Each wore a badge on his vest. Wyatt was an impressive man with blonde hair, a well-groomed mustache, and blue-grey eyes. His slender frame and erect posture made him appear taller than the six feet he stood. Jim was roughly the same height with dark hair and a thick mustache that covered stubborn lines on his thin mouth.

As the men neared the back entrance of the Great Western Hotel, they scanned the area carefully, their hands perched over their pistols, ready to draw if necessary. Fannie Garrettson was crouching near the back door of Mayor James Kelley's home, sobbing.

As Earp and Masterson arrived, her plaintive eyes met theirs and before anyone could speak, she pointed a shaking finger at the house. The men quickly noticed a bullet had splintered the door of the home. They entered Mayor Kelley's place, lifting their six-shooters out of their holsters as they did. A fast inspection of the various rooms of the house led the lawmen to the spot where Dora Hand lay dead.

The two men made their way back outside. They were rattled by the singer's blood-soaked remains, but fixed on the job at hand. ". . . Four shots were fired," Jim offered after a few moments silence, "maybe more." Wyatt bent down next to Fannie and waited for her to gather her composure. "She was sleeping in the Mayor's bed," she said stammering. "He's been sick for two or three weeks and last Monday he was obliged to go to the hospital at the post, Fort Dodge."[2]

The lawmen asked if she had seen the shooter. The grief-stricken woman shook her head. Unable to continue holding back the insistent flood of tears, Fannie broke into more hysterical sobs. The officers waited for the wave of emotion to subside. "What a horrible death," she cried. "To go to bed well and hearty and not dream of anything and be cut down in such a manner, without a chance to breathe a word."[3]

Sympathetic friends of the slain entertainer and of Fannie Garrettson were sent for at the same time as the acting coroner, Judge Refus G. Cook. The distraught singer was escorted to a hotel, and the coroner was shown the deceased.[4]

According to the *Ford County Globe,* October 8, 1878, edition, the mood inside Mayor Kelley's home was heavy and foreboding. Wyatt and Jim, who had now been joined by Bat Masterson, looked on as the judge lifted Dora's arm to inspect the spot where the bullet had entered her body. The judge was a man of medium build with ice-blue eyes that reflected his serious demeanor. He handled her still form with gentleness ordinarily reserved for the living. "Coward," he said under his breath. Bat, a stout, compact man with broad shoulders, dark hair and heavy eyebrows, and a mustache, turned away from the scene and headed into the sitting room, disgusted.

"Kelley know any cowards?" Jim asked, following after his brother. "Hell, he probably serves a dozen or so a night that are all gurgle and no guts," Bat snapped back. "Or maybe," Wyatt interjected, "it's just somebody that can't get served at all at the Alhambra." Bat glanced over at Wyatt, thinking. "Kenedy," he stated matter-of-factly. Wyatt said nothing at first but gave them a moment to consider the notion further.

Over the course of the last four months, James Kenedy had had several run-ins with the law and more than one confrontation with the mayor. On July 29, 1878, Wyatt Earp arrested James for carrying a weapon, and in August, Charlie Bassett had hauled the cattleman into court for disorderly conduct. The charges, penalties, and fines associated with the arrests did not alter James's rebellious behavior.

It only served to fuel the growing hatred he had for law enforcement.[5]

Unaware initially of Mayor Kelley's close association with Dodge City's police force, James had marched into the Alhambra Saloon and Gambling House and began mouthing off about the poor treatment he'd been receiving from the local peace officers. His complaints did not improve the relationship between James and the mayor, which already was an adversarial one.

The matter of a stolen horse Mayor Kelley had purchased from the Kenedy family ranch in Texas had never been resolved. So, when Mayor Kelley approached James and warned him to watch what he said about Sheriff Masterson and his men, it sparked a heated exchange about the integrity of Kenedy's business dealings. The resentful rancher insisted "his kin had bought a bunch of horses from William Bonney in Escatado Country in New Mexico . . . Billy knows his horse flesh," James added curtly. "That fact alone ought to be good and sufficient title enough for any reasonable man."[6]

James's remarks infuriated Mayor Kelley, and he became increasingly outraged when the arrogant cowboy wouldn't stop berating the sheriff and his deputies. The mayor informed him that they were acting under his orders and that "he had damn well better behave himself or get ready for worse treatment." James flew into a rage and attacked Mayor Kelley. The mayor pummeled him and physically ejected him from the saloon. James jerked away from his friends and cohorts who helped him off the ground. He glowered at Mayor Kelley and the men standing behind him laughing, and then he let loose a string of curse words. He ended his tirade with a threat on the mayor's life before throwing himself onto his roan and riding off into the night. It wouldn't be the last time he'd warn Mayor Kelley that he was going to kill him.[7]

Bat's face was set in a scowl as he removed a pocket watch tucked in his vest and fiddled with the gold chain attached to it. He walked toward Dora's room and looked inside. Judge Cook was covering the corpse with a sheet. "He fired the shots from horseback," Wyatt deduced after closely inspecting the bullet holes in the wall. "No one would have known Dora would be in Kelley's bed," Jim added sadly. "Make sure it was Kenedy," Bat forcefully directed while checking his pocket watch. It was shortly after 4:30 a.m. Bat snapped his watch shut as Wyatt and Jim headed out the door.[8]

A pair of horses waiting outside the Long Branch Saloon nickered plaintively as the two lawmen stepped into the establishment. The celebrated tavern presented a brilliant appearance by gaslight. The walls were handsomely decorated, papered, and in the glare of the dazzling light the spectacle was alluring. The favorite resort was thronged all hours of the day and night by liquidators, pasteboard manipulators, stock speculators, and the like.

When they entered the watering hole, Wyatt spotted James Kenedy sitting at a monte table in the back of the room with one of his friends and the dealer. James looked up from the game. He was agitated and trying hard to act like he had nothing to worry about. He slammed down a shot of whisky as he watched the officers find a place at the bar. The bartender, a big man with a square face and a square beard, sauntered over to the pair and asked them what they wanted to drink. "You hear a volley of gunshots a little while ago?" Wyatt inquired. "Came from the direction of the Great Western." The stone-faced bartender swallowed hard and shook his head slightly. He opened a bottle of liquor and poured two drinks—all the while casting quick glances in James's direction. "Was Kenedy outside when the shots were fired?" Wyatt probed patiently. "For God's sake," the bartender said placing the drinks he'd poured in front of the lawmen. "Don't say anything here. Come back to the back room, and I'll tell you."

The bartender grabbed a few empty bottles of alcohol from a shelf and walked to a storage room behind the bar. Wyatt and Jim followed after the man a few moments later. "Spike Kenedy left shortly before the shooting commenced then came back here and ordered a big drink of whisky. I don't know what he was doing, but I do know he figures himself to be immune from ever being arrested again," the bartender told them.

Wyatt stepped out of the back room and looked around for Kenedy, but Kenedy and his friend were gone. The saloon doors were swinging slightly back and forth. The two lawmen ran toward the exit. Out in the street a faint layer of dust danced in the light of the kerosene lamp sitting in the window of the boarding house at the end of the block. The distant hoof beats of a fast-traveling horse climbed and soared in the early morning quiet, then the sound vanished.[9]

"Somebody just leaked out of the landscape," a voice called out from the shadows to Wyatt and Jim, now staring in the direction of the out-of-sight rider. Charlie Bassett, a tall, quiet, well-dressed, clean-shaven man in his early thirties, sauntered over to the pair.

Charlie was the marshal and he was just beginning his morning rounds when he spotted his associates. His face was beaming with friendliness. The men shook hands and Charlie listened intently to the news of Dora's murder and the possible suspect, James Kenedy. "He's always nursed a hatred for the law here," Charlie volunteered. "He hasn't got the backbone to take us on though." Wyatt peered into the night where the rider had disappeared. "Men like that leave a trail that's easy to find," Charlie said noticing Wyatt's worried expression.

A brilliant sun peeked over the horizon and bathed Front Street in a golden early morning light. The greedy cow town was beginning to stir and would soon be preparing once again to gorge itself on the unending stream of money that poured into it. Jim Masterson and Charlie Bassett had fanned out over Dodge and were searching the various businesses for James Kenedy, in case he was still in the area. Deputy Sheriffs William Duffy and Bill Tilghman had joined in the manhunt. Bill, a slim-built, bright-looking twenty-four-year-old, watched the faces of the preoccupied townspeople and cowhands going about their daily routine. He made note of any unusual activity in the alleys and vacant lots and studied the porches and roofs from which suspicious characters might be watching the street. Bat Masterson had taught him the importance of observation. "You look at a town different when you're a sheriff," Bat told him. "You see a lot of things men don't see. Go out there and have a look."[10]

As the news of Dora Hand's murder rolled through Dodge City, Bill saw people's expressions change from polite smiles to preoccupied frowns. Most residents genuinely liked Dora. She proved herself to be a kind and resourceful person who was always ready to help anyone in trouble. One old-timer said of her that "the only thing anyone could hold against her was her after-dark profession, and by Godfrey, I allow she elevated that considerably." [11] Many who had been touched by her generosity and talent came forward with offers to help locate the one responsible for her tragic demise.

A laborer at the stockyards just outside of town, one of Dora's most devoted fans, informed the Dodge City's lawmen of a strange encounter he'd had the day before. A magnificent horse had been delivered at the yard via freight train in the early afternoon on October 3. The man boarded and fed the horse while waiting for the owner's arrival. Nothing out of the ordinary occurred until 3:40 in the morning when he heard a strange noise in the yard and went to investigate. He noticed that one of the saddles left behind by James Kenedy was missing along with the fine horse. Glancing out the exit of the dark yard, he saw the silhouette of a man walking the horse into town. Although he found it peculiar that someone would claim his property at such an early hour, the laborer assumed the slow-moving man was the owner of the ride. [12]

As the man was leading the animal into town, another Dodge City resident happened onto the scene. He was ill and asked the man with the horse if he knew where he might find Dr. McCarty. The man he addressed responded in Spanish, telling the ill man that he didn't speak English.

The man recognized the bluffer to be James Kenedy.

While efforts were being made to locate James, Wyatt Earp was riding fast to Fort Dodge to inform Mayor Kelley of the killing of Dora Hand. Mayor Kelley was recovering from an illness that had plagued him for several weeks. He was a bit pale and weak and the knowledge that Dora was gone drained what color it had from his face. "Bring him in alive, Wyatt," the mayor said, keeping his emotions in check. "Dodge'll want to deal with him as a community."[13]

By the time Wyatt returned to Dodge City with Mayor Kelley, an arrest had been made and an interrogation was in progress. Upon entering the jail the lawman's eyes fell on a disheveled man sitting on a chair in the middle of the room with his hands cuffed.

Wyatt recognized the tired, hungover man as the one he'd seen with James Kenedy at the Long Branch Saloon earlier. Charlie Bassett and William Duffy were leaning against an old wooden desk next to a row of cells, watching Bill Tilghman question the suspect in an even, but forceful manner. Bat Masterson stood behind the man. The weary suspect vehemently denied that he was the shooter or had anything to do with the crime. He insisted that James was the one they wanted. "Kenedy swore that he was going to kill Kelley last night," he blurted.

"Said that the mayor would have to pay." Satisfied the man was telling the truth, the lawmen released him.[14]

The case the lawmen were building against Kenedy was further bolstered when a bartender at the Great Western Hotel came forward with what he knew. He told authorities that the rider he saw leaving the vicinity of the murder was James Kenedy.

A rancher and mercantile owner named Robert Wright delivered more information to the investigating officers about the horse James escorted from the stockyard the night Dora was killed. James and Wright were acquaintances, cattle-men who ran in some of the same circles. He reported that James had been planning the mayor's demise since he was tossed out of Kelley's place during their brawl in August. James made a trip to Kansas City after the fight to give the bruises he received a chance to disappear, and while he was there, he purchased a prize horse. The thoroughbred was rumored to be one of the fastest in the region. James believed the horse would ensure a quick getaway after he killed Mayor Kelley.[15]

Armed with confirmation that James was wholly responsible for killing Dora Hand, the lawmen decided he had to be hunted down and made to answer for the crime.

Judge Cook peered over his wire-rimmed glasses at the line of law enforcement officers entering the courtroom not long after daybreak. Wyatt Earp, Charlie Bassett, Bill Tilghman, and William Duffy were somber and quiet as they peeled off from one another and took seats in the gallery area. A hand-ful of well-groomed jurors milled around the bench, review-ing paperwork and speaking in hushed tones. Bat Masterson was sitting in the witness box, studying a map of the county. Dora Hand's body, which had been brought from the may-or's home, lay rigid on a table near a row of chairs reserved for the coroner's jury. Her form was completely covered by a sheet. Mayor Kelley stood next to her looking heartbro-ken. His eyes transfixed on the outline of her face through the fabric. He was still ailing but could not be persuaded to return to the Fort Dodge infirmary.

In its October 8, 1878, account, the *Ford County Globe* described what occurred next: As the judge made notes on the thick legal document spread out in front of him, he motioned for the jurors to step back. "I have examined the once lovely Dora Hand, who was so foully murdered in her sleep," Judge Cook said in a tone mixed with disappointment and aggravation. "And I've talked with Sheriff Masterson about the shooter. The verdict reads as follows. 'An inquisition holden at Dodge City in said county on the 4th day of October A.D. 1878 before me a Justice of the Peace for Dodge township, said county, acting as coroner on the body of Fannie Keenan [aka Dora Hand], there lying dead, by the jurors whose names are here unto subscribed. Said jurors on their oath do say that Fannie Keenan came to her death by gunshot wound and that in their opinion the said gunshot wound was produced by a bullet discharged from a gun in the hands of one James Kenedy.'"

Once the verdict was read, the men in the courtroom filtered out of the building and into the hectic street. The judge and jurors went their separate ways, back to their homes and businesses. The lawmen, along with Mayor Kelley, continued on together to an eatery. As they walked to the restaurant, citizens stopped to ask them about the shooting and the well-known gunman. Mayor Kelley thoughtfully fielded the queries and promised his constituents that James Kenedy would be brought to justice.

A cast of quick-tempered, unruly cowboys who rode for the Kenedy's King Ranch in Texas watched these inquisitive townspeople flank the mayor and the lawmen at his side.

Although many of the hands thought James Kenedy was hotheaded and egotistical, they were loyal to the brand they rode for and the man who owned it. They disapproved of any law outside of Texas and knew that Kenedy's father would want any attempt to apprehend his son thwarted.[16]

The glares from the King Ranch cowboys did not go unnoticed by Bat, Wyatt, or Bill. They knew James kept company with them and guessed where their allegiance lay.

When they reached the restaurant, all but Wyatt entered. He lingered in the doorway of the business eyeing the zealous cattle pushers. He broke off his gaze, which was rumored to be "able to chill a side of beef," only after he heard the sheriff call for him.

Bat Masterson and his associates surrounded a table filled with sandwiches and coffee. Everyone except Mayor Kelley helped themselves to the food. "This Kenedy party done the shootin' all right," Bat said. "And whether he aimed to kill Dora or whether he was gunning for Kelley and hit her by mistake, doesn't mean anything now." The men discussed the hard riding they would have to do. James had more than an eight-hour head start. "With that kind of a lead," Charlie Bassett noted, "he could make it to the Texas Panhandle before a posse could catch up with him."[17]

The sheriff contemplated the statement for a moment while considering the capable men that were assembled. Whoever set out for James had to be experienced trackers. They had to be riders who could stick in their saddles for days at a time.

Having worked hunting buffalo with Bill Tilghman and Wyatt Earp, he knew they were skilled and resourceful men. "Wyatt Earp is one of the few men I personally knew whom

I regarded as absolutely destitute of physical fear," Bat later wrote about the man. Tilghman was steadfast, an exceptional shot with a rifle, and loyal to the spirit of the law. Bat called him "the greatest of us all." The sheriff knew firsthand the strength of character Charlie Bassett possessed as well. He had worked for Charlie when he was named Dodge City's first sheriff. Bassett's formality in manner and his inborn knowledge of how to get along with people earned him the nickname "Senator." He was at his best when under pressure and had no problem approaching out-of-control men in the midst of a gunfight and disarming them.

A number of men had volunteered to join in the hunt for James Kenedy, but Bat knew the best men for the job were those sitting with him at the table. Mayor Kelley agreed with the sheriff's selection and echoed the sentiments of the *Dodge City Times* newspaper, which, on October 12, 1878, called City Marshal Charlie Bassett, Assistant Marshal Wyatt Earp, Sheriff Bat Masterson, and Deputy Sheriff Bill Tilghman "as intrepid a posse as ever pulled a trigger."

At two o'clock in the afternoon on October 5, the posse loaded their sturdy rides down with their bedrolls, food, guns, and a generous supply of ammunition. Townspeople and ranchers watched the four lawmen prepare for the journey. They wished the men well and took turns shaking their hands.[18]

Fannie Garrettson brushed the lace curtains covering her hotel room window aside and eyed the commotion in the street below. Lines of tears streaked her face. She was tired and still shaken over the violent loss of Dora. She dried her eyes and turned to a small desk beside her bed where a partially written letter was waiting to be finished. Fannie reread what she had jotted down, pausing every now and again to watch the posse get ready for its trip.

"Dear Friends," her letter began. "No doubt ere this you have heard of the very sad and fatal end of Fannie Keenan, one of the most fiendish assassinations on record.

"Although the bullet was not intended for poor Fannie, yet she was the innocent victim, and so it is invariably. Anyone gets it but the one for whom it is intended, and particularly in this wretched city . . . But the man who perpetrated this deed will never exist for a judge or jury, as I have heard the officers have sworn never to take him alive."

Fannie heard the lawmen spur their horses down the street as she dipped her pen into an inkwell to continue the letter. "They have gone in search of the fellows who committed the deed . . . but I am afraid the trouble has not ended, as some twenty of the Texas men will be following after them . . . I want to leave here now, while my life is safe. I think I have had enough of Dodge City."[19]

Fannie concluded her correspondence and set it aside. The pen she had used leaked ink onto the white linen desk cover and left a stain similar to flowing blood. She took another look out the window over the town. The posse had gone. The crowd was slowly dispersing. In the distance a cloud of dust was settling on the rugged trail.

CHAPTER THREE

A Posse on the Move

*She was universally popular among her associates,
and, as one of her acquaintances remarked, "had not
an enemy in the world."*

DODGE CITY TIMES ARTICLE
ABOUT DORA HAND, OCTOBER 5, 1878

Four horsemen thundered out of Dodge City and quickly rode onto the open range. The land before them rolled for miles under a limitless sky. Wyatt Earp and Bill Tilghman held tight to their swift mounts, lagging a few feet behind Bat Masterson and Charlie Bassett. Charlie's roan led the way. Charlie sat forward in his saddle like a mad dog straining against a leash, his eyes fixed on the terrain ahead.

At thirty-one years of age, Charlie Bassett was the oldest among the riders. He had also traveled with more posses than the other men during his five-year law enforcement career in Ford County. He became the county's first sheriff when he was twenty-six years old, and on June 5, 1873, he began the first of three terms in office.[1] He had tracked vigilantes, jewel thieves, and cattle rustlers across Kansas's mostly flat surface, and brought many felons to justice.

Bill Tilghman claimed Bassett's "boyish face belied the steel beneath" and described him as a "steady, level-headed officer who seldom displayed any kind of alarm no matter the crisis."[2]

Whatever Charlie felt about Dora Hand's murder was evident in the way he sat his horse. His legs gripped the back of the animal firmly and he had the reins threaded resolutely through his gloved hands with sufficient lead left over to spank the horse's sides to make the animal go faster. His attentive gaze shifted from the horizon to the trail directly in front of him. He was driven. Charlie liked Dora. He thought she was, as Stuart Lake, the author of the Wyatt Earp biography *Frontier Marshal,* wrote, "the most gracious, beautiful woman to reach Dodge in the heyday of its iniquity."

Charlie had a fine appreciation for Dora's talent as well. She had worked for him on occasion singing at the Long Branch Saloon, an establishment he opened shortly after he arrived in Dodge. The Long Branch, named after a celebrated sporting resort on the Atlantic seaboard, was the largest and most profitable saloon in the region. As an East Coast native himself, Charlie was familiar with the popular original. One critic called his Dodge City saloon "artistically functional . . . It offered a little of everything: a lengthy bar, gaming tables, music, entertainment, and dancing. On busy nights the swinging doors were kept open to expedite the traffic." The doors were kept open every time Dora played the Long Branch.

Having a second job as saloon owner wasn't uncommon for a lawman at the time. The risks associated with upholding the law were great and the rewards, especially the pay, were minimal. Charlie's salary was $100 a month. Men like Wyatt Earp and Bat Masterson took on work defending the law in between gambling and mining projects. Being a lawman was a full-time occupation for very few.[3]

Prior to entering law enforcement, Charlie served in the military. He enlisted in the Union Army in 1865 and served in the 213th Pennsylvania Infantry. He was ordered to Washington, D.C., placed on garrison duty, and honorably discharged after serving only nine months in the military. He migrated west, settling in Dodge City in early 1872, and initially made his living as a buffalo hunter and cattleman. The thriving cow town had a reputation as "hell on the frontier," and Charlie saw it as a place where he could make money from the thirsty cowboys driving their herds into the area.[4]

Charlie ran an orderly saloon. He didn't tolerate gunplay and often chased violent offenders out of his business. He had a quiet but forceful presence and nerves of steel, and although he didn't have a reputation as a gunfighter, he was good with a pistol and wasn't shy about using it if provoked. He was known throughout the territory as a "brave and honest man." When the city founders decided they needed a sheriff to keep the peace, Charlie was the first one they asked to wear the badge. During his many years in law enforcement, he served as sheriff and under sheriff of Dodge City, and marshal and deputy marshal for Ford County.

Sheriff Bassett's authority covered a large portion of territory. His name frequently appeared in Dodge City newspapers accompanying stories about the apprehending of bandits who waged war against law-abiding citizens. On March 31, 1877, a *Dodge City Times* article reported on his pursuit of a desperado who had made off with a dozen horses: "A slight horse-thief scare pervaded this morning," the story read. "From what we learn it appears that twelve horses were missing from Mr. J. W. Miller's cattle camp on Crooked yesterday. Supposing they had been stolen, the authorities were informed, and Sheriff Bassett and Marshall Lawrence E. Deger started out this morning to see what they could find. About three miles west of town they discovered the horses, but no thieves were in sight."

The criminals Sheriff Bassett pursued were not limited to horse thieves. In September 1877, he set out to bring in a train and stage robber from Texas named Sam Bass. Bass and five other men had held up a Union Pacific train in Big Springs, Nebraska, and made off with sixty thousand dollars. It was reported that the bandits were headed for Dodge City and a wire was sent to Sheriff Bassett to let him know.

The *Dodge City Times* reported that "as soon as preparations could be made, Bassett, Bat Masterson and Under Sheriff John Webb started southwest on horseback, intending to try to intercept the robbers if possible. Assistant Marshal Ed Masterson and Deputy Sheriff (Miles) Mix went west the same day to find out what they could about the men who crossed the road. They could learn nothing of any importance except that the men had been seen on Thursday morning, but no one had taken particular notice of them. Masterson and Mix returned the same evening. Nothing has been heard from Sheriff Bassett and his men since they started from here yesterday morning."

Ultimately Sheriff Bassett was unable to catch Bass, but his posse did manage to help drive Bass and his gang out of the state.

Dodge City had an ordinance that prohibited firearms from being carried in town and Charlie frequently interceded when cowboys did not comply with the rule. On one such occasion, the sheriff was called to the scene of a heated dispute—at the Long Branch saloon—between two men who had not surrendered their weapons. The men involved in the ruckus, Frank Loving and Levi Richardson, stood on either side of the tavern firing at one another. When Sheriff Bassett arrived, Richardson had been seriously injured and Loving was still shooting at him. Without hesitating Charlie marched through the thick gun smoke and smattering of bullets to Loving and jerked the pistol out of his hand.

Bassett's account of the incident was just as composed as his actions. "When I first heard the firing I was at Beatty and Kelley's saloon," the sheriff later testified. "I ran up to the Long Branch as fast as I could. Saw Frank Loving, Levi Richardson and Duffey [William Duffey was a deputy sheriff]. Richardson was dodging and running around the billiard table. Loving was also running and dodging around the table. I got as far as the stove when the shooting had about ended. I caught Loving's pistol. Think there was two shots fired after I got into the room, am positive there was one."[5]

In yet another barroom altercation, Charlie was called upon to disarm the victor of a fatal argument. Artista H. Webb had bashed in Barney Martin's skull with the butt of his Winchester rifle and was attempting to get away when Charlie intervened. According to the September 9, 1879, edition of the *Ford County Globe*, "Bassett seized him [Webb] and took away his rifle, which was found to be loaded and cocked. He was first taken to the calaboose, but a crowd gathering quickly, among whom were some who favored lynching, the sheriff deemed it prudent to remove the prisoner to the county jail."

The *Globe* gave Sheriff Bassett high praise for his "vigilance and prompt action in the arrest of offenders of the law." Citizens called him a "cool and fearless officer."

A number of incidents leading up to Dora's murder in October 1878 tested the sheriff's steady composure. In January, Charlie, Bat Masterson, and several other members of a posse tracked down a gang of violent train robbers. One of the desperados was the notorious Dave Rudabaugh. Rudabaugh and his accomplices were held over for trial. Rudabaugh was later released after informing on his cohorts, left the area, and teamed up with Billy the Kid.

Three months after the Rudabaugh incident, Ed Masterson, the kind and amiable marshal of Dodge City, was shot and killed. Masterson's death drove city officials to beef up law enforcement. Rebellious cowboys and some indignant taxpayers were livid about the "army of police" hired to provide extra security. Texans irate over the strict enforcement of the law against firearms and disturbing the peace in the Kansas town offered $1,000 to any man who "killed Wyatt Earp and helped ease restrictions on a trail hand's need to raise hell."[6]

In spite of the additions to the force, a second policeman, Deputy Marshal H. T. McCarty was gunned down at the Long Branch Saloon in July. A week later, a Texas herder on a shooting spree through town was shot and killed by Marshal Wyatt Earp and policeman Jim Masterson. In September, Cheyenne Indian leader Dull Knife fled the reservation and led his band of followers across western Kansas to their ancestral home in the Black Hills of the Dakotas. Charlie Bassett and other members of the police force were on hand to help keep order and protect homesteaders from possible raids by the Cheyenne.

The killing of Dora Hand was considered by many in the territory to have been the most shocking of all the violent events that occurred in Dodge in 1878. Dora's assassin, James Kenedy, was well known to all the peace officers in town. He had a penchant for troublemaking and had been hauled into court numerous times. Like his cohorts, Charlie found the cattle baron to be a "reckless braggart." He wasn't the typical range hand. His father, Capt. Mifflin Kenedy, and rancher Richard King had combined their holdings to create a massive cattle conglomerate that brought thousands of dollars in business to Dodge City every year. The Kenedy-King outfit drove more than fifteen thousand head of longhorns through Ford County in 1878 alone.

James always took full advantage of the influence his family's money generated. He was in one scrape after another in nearly every cow town he passed through from Ellsworth, Kansas, to Santa Fe, New Mexico. Whether he was shooting up saloons just for the hell of it or challenging cardsharps to gunfights, he generally walked away from the situation without injury or paying a severe penalty.

In hopes that his son would settle down, the "Captain" purchased acreage in Tascosa, Texas, and filled it with two thousand head of cattle and a ranching crew and gave it to James to run. James's wild ways subsided for a while, but not for long.

James Kenedy's good friend Dr. Henry F. Hoyt wrote in his memoirs that "in the course of time he [Kenedy] drove a herd to Dodge City, Kansas, sold them, and, unable to withstand the temptations of the underworld there, he stepped out." Dr. Hoyt also described James as "a wild one." The men were close friends and both spent a lot of time together at the gambling tables. Dr. Hoyt's red hair and a fair complexion contrasted James's dark features and dark hair, and it was for that reason the pair were dubbed "the roulette twins."

Shooting Dora Hand was just one of the many crimes James committed in his life. Born into wealth on February 22, 1855, his Mexican mother and Pennsylvania-bred father, a former steamboat captain, raised James and his eleven siblings to respect the family name and expect nothing less from any other man. James seemed to spend much of his life dishonoring the Kenedy handle, while demanding a reverence for it from everyone else. One of the first serious run-ins he had with the law came about because he was defending the Kenedy honor.

On July 20, 1872, James was engaged in a card game at the Lentz saloon in Ellsworth, Kansas, with four other men. All hell broke loose when James, notorious for dealing from the bottom of the deck, accused a fellow Texas rancher of cheating. The rancher, Print Olive, was unarmed and could not draw on James, who was aching for a fight. As Olive stormed out of the saloon, James promised that there would be "another day." Before sunset James was combing the streets of Ellsworth looking for Olive.

James found Olive at a billiard saloon playing poker. The brash Kenedy sauntered over to the cattle rancher unnoticed by the other unsuspecting patrons around him. "You son-of-a-bitch," James shouted. "Now you can cash in your checks!" James quickly pulled his gun and fired three shots at Olive. An associate of Olive's intervened and shot James in the leg, bringing the gunplay to an abrupt halt.[7]

News of the incident made the front page of the August 1, 1872, edition of the *Ellsworth Reporter.* "Ellsworth which has been remarkably quiet this season, had its first shooting affair this season last Saturday at about six o'clock, at the Ellsworth Billiard saloon. The room was full of 'money changers' at the time, busily at work, and lookers on intently watching the games. Among others I. P. Olive was seated at a table playing cards.

"All of a sudden a shot was heard and sooner than we can write it, four more shots were fired. Kennedy *[sic]* came into the room, went behind the bar and taking a revolver walked up in front of Olive and fired at him telling him to 'pass the checks.' Olive threw up his hands exclaiming 'don't shoot.' The second, third and fourth shots took effect, one entering the groin and making a bad wound, one in the thigh and one in the hand.

"Olive could not fire, though he was armed, but someone, it seems uncertain who, fired at Kenedy, hitting him in the hip, making only a flesh wound. The difficulty arose from a game of cards in the forenoon. Kenedy accused Olive of unfair dealing. Olive replied in language that professionals cannot bear. The affair made considerable excitement. The wounded were taken in custody and cared for by Drs. Duck and Fox. They extracted the bullet from Olive and a piece of gold watch chain, which was shot into the wound. It was feared that Olive would not survive, but the skill of the doctors saved him. Kenedy was removed to South Main Street and put under the guard of three policemen, but with the aid of friends he escaped during the night from the window and has not been heard from. All has been quiet since the affair and is likely to remain so."[8]

James kept company with fellow Texans John Goodman, Peter Murchinson, and Ben Thompson, outlaws who dabbled in the cattle business and who, on more than one occasion, helped each other escape prosecution for their misdeeds.

In late 1875 James was offered an opportunity to serve as a Texas Ranger. As such, he would fight against the frustrated Indians in the area, help prevent Mexican bandits from stealing livestock, and oversee disputes between warring range families. He jumped at the chance. The Ranger command was based in the heart of Texas's Nueces County. The sprawling Kenedy family ranch was located in the area, and James knew the region well. The job proved to be too tame for him, however, and in April 26, 1876, he was discharged at his own request.[9] He returned to his ranch in Tascosa and divided his time between wrangling cattle and gambling. He was involved in numerous barroom altercations prior to finding trouble in Dodge City. It wasn't until he laid eyes on Dora Hand that he began to seriously contemplate changing his ways.

As the intrepid posse charged along the Old Santa Fe Trail in search of James Kenedy, the editors of the Dodge City newspapers were setting the type for the morning edition. PISTOL DOES ITS WORK was the headline across the Saturday,

October 5, 1878, edition of the *Dodge City Times*. The concise and unbiased article ended by assuring citizens that "officers were in pursuit of the supposed murderer, to whom circumstances pointed very directly."

Charlie watched the festering clouds ahead as he rode hard. The long, wavy billows were vaguely reminiscent of the profile of Dora's face under the white sheet that the coroner had draped over her. A far-off clap of thunder jerked him out of this reverie and prompted him to slow his horse to a stop. The other riders followed suit. The men dismounted near a thin row of cottonwood trees lining the banks of the Arkansas River. The horses, lathered and sweating, wandered to the water's edge and sunk their noses into the river. The posse brushed off some of the thick dust that covered them from head to foot and took a long drink from their canteens.

"What do you think, Senator?" Bat asked after surveying their surroundings. "My guess . . . he's heading back to his place in Tascosa," Charlie replied, giving the ground around him a once over. "Taking the Jones and Plummer Trails to the Texas Panhandle all the way home. And seeing how he's on a horse without shoes it's going to be harder to track him."[10]

Bat and the two other men partially agreed with Charlie. The fact that Kenedy's horse wasn't shod would make it difficult to pick up his trail. There was some doubt that he was going to return to Texas using the standard route. Bat speculated that Kenedy might be on his way to Cheyenne. He'd bragged to his associates that he "had people there that would help him if he ever needed it," and he was last seen heading west when he left Dodge. Wyatt and Bill had a hunch the outlaw was only pretending to head toward Wyoming. They believed he would take a different road back to Texas and avoid the routinely traveled pathways. "I think he'll cut over the Texas Trail into the Indian nation," Bill offered. "Then double back and cross the ford in the river near Wagon Bend Springs." Wyatt nodded his head in agreement. "Then we've got to get to the Cimarron River before he does," Charlie said flatly.[11]

One by one the men collected their horses and mounted up. A sunset was heavy in the sky as they slapped leather and their rides cantered off. With the exception of Wyatt, they all fell into step together. Wyatt turned his horse around and stared expectantly over the plot of land they had covered. There was a sense that he might see something moving in the far horizon but nothing stirred. Satisfied that they weren't being followed, he whipped his ride around and hurried off to rejoin the posse.

On the very outskirts of Dodge City, twenty Texas cowboys poured out onto the prairie. Among them were Dr. Henry Hoyt and several friends and employees of the King Ranch. They were a purposeful group, heavily armed and wearing serious, determined expressions.

CHAPTER FOUR

THUNDER OVER THE PRAIRIE

*Drunks are rolled, men are found dead on the street,
our women are not safe, and highway robberies are
constantly committed in spite of the expensive police
force in Dodge.*

A COMPLAINT LISTED IN THE
DODGE CITY TIMES, MAY 1878

A crowd of Texas trail hands watched the prairie hurry past them as they pressed their rides into a full gallop. A train racing in the opposite direction issued a long blast from its whistle that floated over miles of grassy fields. Dr. Henry Hoyt, part-time cowboy and physician for the King Ranch, was out in front of the riders, an unlit cigar was clamped tightly between his jaws. Like the others on horseback riding with him, he was dressed in the rough clothing of the cattle trail. His tall hat was pushed back from his sunburned face. When he and his cohorts left Dodge City, they had in mind to intercept the posse pursuing James Kenedy and give the wealthy cattleman a chance to get out of the territory safely. Shortly after they started on their way, it was decided they should return to the ranch in southern Texas and inform James's father about the incident involving his son.

The King Ranch, located between Corpus Christi and Brownsville, sprawled across six Texas counties, for more than 1,280 miles. Hundreds of hands worked the spread. Dr. Hoyt suspected that when Mifflin Kenedy learned about the trouble James was in, he would dispatch a legion of dutiful men, indignant over the harsh treatment of a fellow Texan. Hundreds of discontented cowboys who believed their occasional illegal actions deserved a free pass because of the wages they spent in Dodge would go to great lengths to champion one of their kind. Dr. Hoyt knew this and knew that Captain Kenedy was aware of it as well. Mifflin's organized efforts on behalf of his son would be more effective than twenty-five or thirty rogue hands acting independently. It was with that thought in mind that Dr. Hoyt and friends headed off in the direction of the Chisholm Trail toward home.[1]

A cold wind hissed through the cracks of the walls and doors of a sprawling, dilapidated mud-and-wood store near a place called Mulberry Crossing, twenty-seven miles south of Dodge City. With the exception of an inebriated trail hand, the dusty stretch in front of the business was deserted and still. A weathered sign over the entrance read, A. H. DUGAN, OWNER.[2]

Dugan, a heavy-set man who had sagging jowls and thinning black hair combed across his sweaty scalp, ran the stage stop that was a combination mercantile and saloon. He was wiping a rugged wood table with a mop rag when Bat Masterson and Bill Tilghman entered. Three riders with the look of seasoned cattlemen and the sound of Texas in their voices were seated in the back of the room and looked up from their poker game when the police officers entered. The tension in the air was almost visible.

The cowboys continued on with their game as Bat and Bill meandered over to the bar. "It's two bits for a bucket of water for your horses," Dugan said, blowing the dust off a can of peaches and putting it back on the shelf. "We're looking for someone who might have come by here," Bat stated. "It's still two bits," Dugan replied, unimpressed. The lawmen politely explained who they were looking for and described James Kenedy. Dugan told them no one who looked like Kenedy had been through. "And I would know," he added. "I know every teamster, trail hand, and stage driver that passes by."[3]

Bat turned his attention to the men playing cards. The cowboys were too engrossed with their hands to care.

Dugan told the officers that the ranchers were part of a nearby spread and had come in to load up on provisions and decided to stay for a game and a bottle. Satisfied with the response, Bat and Bill turned to leave. "What did this fellow do?" Dugan asked before the men reached the door. Bill told him that he'd shot a woman in Dodge. "She was a singer," he elaborated. "Her name was Dora Hand."

Dugan's expression fell. He removed a bottle of cheap liquor from under the counter and poured himself a drink. "Damn shame," he said sadly as he lifted the glass to his lips. "My sister dragged me to the Union church some months back," Dugan confessed. "Miss Hand sang a solo. Prettiest thing I ever did hear."[4] The gruff businessman hummed a bit of the hymn he was recalling before asking Bill if he had known Dora. "Yes," Bill kindly answered, "I knew her." Before exiting the building, Bat warned Dugan and his patrons not to say anything about their passing through. "When you find the murderer, I hope you kill him," Dugan snapped. "It may come to that," Bat replied.

Wyatt and Charlie, who had been surveying the area around the primitive store, hopped aboard their horses at the same time Bat and Bill mounted up. Charlie let them know they hadn't had any luck finding Kenedy's tracks.

"I think we need to get a wire to the Sheriff of Cheyenne," Bat said adjusting himself in the saddle. "We've been through this, Bat," Charlie announced. "Kenedy's talk about Wyoming is a blind," Bill added, looking over the landscape. "He followed the Arkansas River way west and is going to cut across the Texas Trail and rejoin the Jones and Plummer Trail to get to the shallowest spot on the Cimmaron."[5] Bat resisted arguing with them further and led the riders back onto the wide-open plains. "Kenedy's caught in his own loop," Charlie interjected. "That's about all there is of him. He doesn't have none of his old Daddy, that's why he'll run home to him."[6]

Bill brought up the rear of the posse, his mind on the pursuit, the lateness of the day, and Dora Hand. "Half the population [of Dodge] were gamblers or prostitutes," Bill wrote to his wife Zoe, in 1877. "The prostitutes were painted up like a present day respectable woman, and looked mighty pretty in their satins and laces." Dora was among those "painted ladies" he found appealing when drifting across the stage in her stylish fineries. There were some Dodge City residents who suggested she was a soiled dove, but female entertainers west of Independence, Missouri, were often viewed as harlots by the general population.

As part owner of the Crystal Palace Saloon, Bill would have welcomed an attraction like Dora at his establishment. Soiled dove or not, her name and talent meant increased business. Regardless of her profession he saw her murder as a tragic event and one that needed to be atoned for.

William Matthew Tilghman Jr.'s drive to legitimately right a wrong began at an early age at Fort Dodge, Iowa. Born on the 4th of July 1854 to an army soldier turned farmer, and a young homemaker, Bill spent his early childhood in the heart of the Sioux Indian territory in Minnesota. Grazed by an arrow when he was a baby, he was raised to respect Native Americans and protect his family from tribes that felt they had been unfairly treated by the government. Bill was one of six children. His mother insisted he had been "born to a life of danger."

In 1859 his family moved to a homestead near Atkinson, Kansas. While Bill's father and oldest brother were off fighting in the Civil War, he worked the farm and hunted game. One of the most significant events in his life occurred when he was twelve years old while returning home from a blackberry hunt. His hero Marshal Bill Hickok (Wild Bill) rode up beside him and asked if he had seen a man ride through with a team of mules and a wagon.

The wagon and mules had been stolen in Abilene and the marshal had pursued the culprit across four hundred miles. Bill told Hickok that the thief had passed him on the road that led to Atkinson. The marshal caught the criminal before he left the area and escorted him back to the scene of the crime. Bill was so taken by Hickok's passion for upholding the law he decided to follow in his footsteps and become a scout and lawman.

Bill Tilghman set out on his own in 1871 and became a buffalo hunter. Using the Sharps rifle his father had given him, the eighteen-year-old learned the trade quickly and was an exceptional shot. He secured a contract with the railroad's owners to provide workers laying tracks to Fort Dodge, Kansas, and the subsequent town that grew close to it, Dodge City, with buffalo meat.

From September 1, 1871, to April 1, 1872, Bill killed and delivered three thousand buffalo. He set an all-time record, surpassing the previous one made by Wild Bill Hickok. Bill Tilghman's success as a buffalo hunter was due in part to his relationship with the Plains Indians. He never invaded their hunting grounds and treated them with a dignity and reverence not commonly displayed by white men.

Bill's extensive knowledge of the territory prompted cattle barons like Matt Childers to hire him to round up his livestock roaming about the area and then drive them to the market at Dodge. He was exceptional at the job, but his true ambition was to become a law enforcement officer. He was a natural at settling disputes between friends and competitors engaged in heated arguments, a necessity for any policeman. Army colonels and other high-ranking military leaders wanting help settling differences between themselves and angry Native Americans sought out Bill. Although he would not wage war with the Indians against the United States, he did understand their bitter feeling toward the white men. In hopes of driving the Cheyenne, Crow, and Blackfoot out of the country, the government ordered that their main source of food be slaughtered. The mighty buffalo was hunted to near extinction.

With the buffalo gone, Bill was forced to find other employment. From 1873 to 1878, he worked as a merchant, contractor, land speculator, horse racer, cavalry scout, and livery stable and saloon owner. He ran the Crystal Palace with his business partner, Henry Garris.

The Palace was located on the south side of Dodge City and refinements to the tavern made the news on July 21, 1877. According to the *Dodge City Times,* "Garris and Tilghman's Crystal Palace is receiving a new front and an awning, which will tend to create a new attraction towards the never ceasing fountains of refreshments flowing within." Bill also owned and operated a ranch thirteen miles outside of Dodge, one that he would never relinquish.

As a proprietor of the Crystal Palace, some of the customers he befriended had questionable and sometimes criminal backgrounds. It was guilt by association that led to his arrest on suspicion of being one of the notorious Kinsley train robbers. On February 9, 1878, the *Dodge City Times* reported that "William Tilghman, a citizen of Dodge City, was arrested on the same serious charge of attempt to rob the train. He stated he was ready for trial, but the State asked for 10 days delay to procure witnesses, which was granted. Tilghman gave bail. It is generally believed that William Tilghman had no hand in the attempted robbery." The charges were dismissed four days after the arrest.

Two months later, Bill was arrested for horse theft. A pair of stolen horses found at his livery implicated him in the crime. A thorough investigation proved that he had not been involved, as reported in the April 23, 1878, edition of the *Ford County Globe.*

In the spring of 1877, he married widow Flora Kendall and moved her and her baby to his Bluff Creek Ranch. Tilghman was now a respected family man and cattleman in Ford County. When Bat Masterson was elected sheriff of Dodge City in early 1878, one of his first orders of business was to hire Bill on as his deputy. In spite of Bill's encounters with the law, he was certain the esteemed Tilghman would be a positive addition to the force. Bat knew about Bill's reputation with a gun and his knowledge of Kansas and the surrounding territory. He also knew Bill didn't drink, which meant there'd never be a question of alcohol affecting his judgment. "I've seen many a man get killed just because his hand was a little unsteady or slow on the draw, when he had a few drinks in him," Bill maintained.[7]

As a lawman, Bill honed the art of reading people's faces, attitudes, and gestures. He could spot a "two-bit crook" from a law-abiding citizen at a glance. He believed that "God Almighty never made a crook, but he put his mark on him." Bat and Bill had their work cut out for them establishing order in Dodge. "Every time a bunch of liquored-up cowhands ride into town on a Saturday night to shoot it up, they hurt innocent people," Sheriff Masterson told Bill. "The merchants want this stopped. They don't want the saloons closed down, they want cowpunchers to come in and spend their money, but they want the gunplay stopped."[8]

Bill was dedicated to his position and approached his law enforcement duties, which included maintaining the office and records, feeding prisoners, and the supervision of the jail, with quiet determination. He wasn't content with solely keeping the peace; he wanted to know all about the legal process and proper methods of gathering evidence. Ford County prosecutor Mike Sutton taught Bill the finer points of the law, and he emerged from the education a true authority on the legal process.

Unlike his mentors Bat Masterson and Charlie Bassett, and his idol, Bill Hickok, who focused primarily on apprehending criminals using any means possible, Bill challenged himself to work within the confines of the law. Friend and foe alike appreciated his due diligence.

Bill believed a "man never set out to do anything wrong, he convinced himself that he was right first." James Kenedy didn't set out to do anything wrong. He thought his vendetta was a righteous one.[9]

Twelve hours after he killed Dora Hand, Kenedy was on the run and being pursued by men who knew the creeks, ranches, and the wildernesses beyond Dodge City better than some of the natives. The posse would hunt him down. Bill told his fellow riders, "We'll find him, it's just a matter of when. That's the way I see it."

The posse rode hard for hours heading in the direction of Meade Centre (later called Meade City). Always looking for signs of the criminal they were after, their eyes swept the horizon without detecting any evidence of habitation. There was nothing but the brown trail in front of them and the grassy prairie land on either side of it for as far as the eye could see. Clusters of trees standing near creeks that ran through the region provided the only shade from the sun or protection available from torrential downpours. A few small prairie dog towns on the high flats were oases for weary travelers. They were life-saving stops because they supplied food, water, and shelter for riders tired of the monotony of the scenery. If, as the posse believed, James Kenedy circled back, he would ride to the main thoroughfare used by pioneers, freighters, and cattle drovers and end up at one of the minuscule, but often necessary, stops.

In the area of a prairie dog town near the future site of the town of Kismet, Kansas, Wyatt Earp spotted the muddy prints of an unshod horse.[10] The sun was setting, and the fast-approaching night sky combined with ominous dark storm clouds hampered their attempt to follow a promising lead. Lightning streaked overhead, thunder boomed, and a heavy rain quickly drenched the men. They removed slickers from their saddlebags and pulled them tightly around their shoulders. Leading their skittish rides to a projecting stream bank, the men huddled together with the horses, trying to protect themselves from the driving showers slowly turning to hail. Wyatt watched the fragments of the prints he found wash away, and he cursed the elements under his breath.

The tempest raged over the entire southwestern part of the state. Like the posse, James was suffering through the storm as well. He'd found a slight outcropping of earth situated between two hills and burrowed into the loose dirt. He pulled his saturated hat around his ears and jerked on the reins of his horse, inching the animal closer to him, blocking the blowing, freezing rain. Although he could barely see his hand in front of his face because of the downpour, he knew he was somewhere in the middle of Seward County, close to Ford County. If the weather cooperated, he expected to cross the Cimarron River the following day.

After managing to keep off the usual trails running in to and out of Dodge, he drifted back on the route close to Meade Centre. James anticipated that the law would be out for him. At a stage stop the day before, he'd asked about the posse, but no one admitted to seeing any police in the vicinity. He left the trail again, zigzagging through the area, hoping to shake the posse off his route. He wanted to rest, but he couldn't close his eyes for fear that he'd miss trail hands from his Tascosa Ranch he was sure would be searching for him. Given the constant rain, it seemed unlikely they'd be riding, but he thought there might be a chance. The wind moaned fitfully. He wiped the rain from his face and shifted his position on the wet ground. "He had it coming," James reminded himself aloud about Mayor Kelley. His eyes were heavy and against his will, he dropped off to sleep.

CHAPTER FIVE

CAUGHT IN A STORM

The murderer was a fiend in human form . . . this man has been allowed more privileges than the rest of them because he has plenty of money, and now he has repaid their liberality.

FANNIE GARRESTSON'S COMMENTS
ABOUT THE MAN WHO MURDERED DORA HAND, 1878

A pile of coal-black thunderclouds unleashed a torrent of cold rain on the posse's crude camp. The canvas lean-to tied to boulders jutting out of the bank of a stream sagged with the weight of the water. Lightning pulsated, reflecting off the faces of the four lawmen waiting out the storm. They were tired but resolute. The turmoil of wind blew rain into their poor excuse for shelter and splashed off their hats and slickers. "If any of you know where that ark is tied up, you might want to make your way for it now," Bat said jokingly, raising his voice over the weather. His fellow riders chuckled politely as he removed a soggy cigar from the breast pocket of his coat. He played with the wet stogie for a minute trying to convince himself that it could be lit.

All at once any attempt to fire it up seemed foolish, and he threw the cigar down on the ground beside him. "Damn it all," he said folding his arms across his chest.

None of the men were surprised by the water-logged conditions. The hot, dry Kansas summers could blister the paint off any building, and the wet, cold winters that followed behind could scour blistered paint down to raw timbers. Prairie fires ignited by lightning scorched everything in their path and flash floods carried all the debris away. Members of the intrepid posse had experienced all that the territory's harsh seasons offered. The forces of nature had shaped them and made them more resilient. They drifted in and out of fitful sleep, hoping each time they opened their eyes that the relentless rain would have stopped, and they could be on their way.

"The Lord sure must have pulled the cork," Bat said when noticing everyone was struggling to drop off. "I rode in rain like this for six days," Bill said after giving Bat's comment a decent moment of thought. "I was driving a herd of cattle for Mart Childers through Cheyenne country."

The conversation was a welcome distraction from their attempts at slumber. Charlie, Wyatt, and Bat focused their attention on Bill. "The prairie sod was a quagmire," he continued. "The horses hooves sank ankle-deep in the mud. Heading north in the sloshing rain was slow going . . . and then we spotted Kicking Bird and his braves watching us through the rain."[1]

Charlie coolly scanned their immediate surroundings remembering that the Plains Indians could have their eyes fixed on them at the moment as well. Bill told the men about his riding partner, Hurricane Martin. He and Hurricane stood alone against fifty warring Cheyenne. The braves attempted to flank the cowboys on either side by dividing into two groups. Bill and Hurricane urged their horses into full gallops to try and outrun them. The rain-soaked terrain made fast travel close to impossible not only for Bill and his friend, but also for the pursuing Indians.

The thirteen cow ponies Bill had tied together raced beside them as best as they could. Some carried packs filled with supplies. As the race wore on and the Indians began to close in on the cowboys, Bill and Hurricane were forced to cut the ropes tethering the animals to their mounts. The loose steeds did not slow the Cheyenne down as Bill had expected. They merely split up again and one Indian remained behind with the pack horses. The warriors hurried on after the cowboys.

Hurricane tried to persuade Bill to stop and shoot at the braves, but moving as fast as they were, Bill determined he'd only be able to inflict minimum damage. "Killing one wouldn't do any good, and it'd just make the rest of them want revenge," Bill shouted to Hurricane.

The war party eventually split into three, one group charged up the middle and the other two rode to the right and left. The braves chased the cowboys up a steep hill leaving them with no easy way out. The only possible means of escape was to head straight down the other side of the summit. At the bottom of the sixty-foot cliff was a fast-flowing stream. Hurricane suggested that he and Bill kill their horses and use them as barricades while fighting off the Cheyenne. Bill disapproved of the idea pointing out that they didn't have enough ammunition to do the job. The memory of the scalped and mutilated surveyors and buffalo hunters he'd seen in his life came flooding into Bill's mind. Fear and anger churned in his stomach. "We're going over the cliff," Bill told Hurricane.

After forcing their rides down the dangerous embankment, the cowboys followed suit. The horses and riders survived the jump, but they were battered and bruised and came close to drowning in the rain-swollen creek.

By the time the men got to their feet and were leading the animals to safety, Kicking Bird and his warriors had reached the top of the summit. Bill grabbed his gun and shot at them. The Indians dismounted and flattened themselves against the rocks. They didn't return fire, and they didn't pursue the men over the cliff.

Bill's reminiscences momentarily lightened the spirits of the sleep-deprived posse. For a brief time the wet conditions were only a minor irritation. Charlie pulled the collar of his slicker tight around his neck and grinned as he shared his own tale of battling the elements while tracking a band of renegades known as the Collins Gang.[2] Two members of the group, the notorious Sam Bass and another man named Davis, tried to flee the Kansas in a horse and buggy after robbing a train. Charlie was fast on their trail when a lightning storm blasted through the area. Heavy drops of rain crashed down on the lawman and the posse he was riding with. Soldiers dispatched from Fort Dodge to assist in the pursuit were caught in the deluge as well.

Charlie and his men and the soldiers had divided up to be more effective in capturing the bandits, but when the rain made it impossible to go on, all three groups made camp.

The manhunt remained at a standstill until the unsettled weather passed. Seeking shelter from the violent bluster, Bass and Davis wandered into the soldiers' camp. Unaware of whom the innocent looking men were, the troops invited them to share their fire and provisions. The outlaws entertained the men with lively stories they said they'd heard about the Collins Gang—stories that included details of various robberies. The following morning, the soldiers and the bandits parted company. "They sent them on their way . . . even wished them good luck in their endeavors," Charlie told Wyatt, Bat, and Bill.

Charlie's story was followed by one from Wyatt about wintering on the Salt Fork of the Arkansas River with Bat Masterson and his brother Ed. He described the mountain-like snowdrifts piled outside the dugout where they spent their evenings as "deep enough to lose a man in."[3] The three men were buffalo hunters at the time and had followed the herd to the canyons around southern Kansas containing the grass they existed on during the winter. The trio made good money off the animals. The buffalo robe business was huge. Hides were worth $35 each and the meat sold for ten cents a pound.

It was bitter cold and the vast prairie was unmarked by any lines of a traveled road. The air was full of driving snowstorms and temperatures dipped down to twenty degrees below zero. "The only thing that took the chill off was the rotgut whisky from those rolling saloons that would pull into the camps near us," Bat recalled, joining in the storytelling.[4]

When the conversation slowly died to nothing, the sound of the continuing rain filled the quiet again. Bat rested his head on a smooth rock in the wall of the creek bank and inconspicuously rubbed the front of his legs as though they had fallen asleep, and he was trying to wake them. On January 24, 1876, he'd been involved in a gunfight that left him with a lifelong injury, one that caused his legs to ache and forced him to use a cane when he walked.

Bat was twenty-three years old and enjoying time away from hunting buffalo in a bawdy range town in Texas called

Mobeetie. After spending the evening at the gambling tables at a dance hall called the Lady Gay, Bat retired to his room with a young woman named Mollie Brennan. Sgt. Melvin A. King, one of the men with whom he had been playing cards, was furious with Bat over what he perceived as "underhanded dealings."[5]

With a loaded six-gun in hand, King pounded on Bat's hotel room door and waited for him to answer. Assuming it was his friends wanting him to join them for a nightcap, Bat unlocked the door. Sergeant King burst into the room and opened fire. Mollie came between Bat and one of the bullets and was critically wounded. Bat was shot in the pelvis, but he managed to grab his gun and kill King before collapsing.

In spite of his best efforts, the local physician could not save Mollie. An army surgeon was called to the scene to remove the bullet from Bat's lower midsection and stayed with him until he recovered. Bat would walk with a limp for the rest of his life, but he used the cane that aided his walking his advantage. On more than one occasion Bat subdued opponents with the staff, cracking them in the head to get their attention or across their gun hand to disarm them. "Even as a cripple, he was a first class peace officer," Wyatt Earp boasted of his friend.[6]

Bartholomew Masterson was born on November 26, 1853, near Montreal, Canada. His parents, Thomas Masterson and Catherine McGurk, were farmers who immigrated to Illinois in 1861. They continued to trek west until they reached Kansas and settled on a 160-acre spread northeast of Wichita.

The Mastersons had seven children, five boys and two girls. Bartholomew was the second to the oldest and was the most sturdy and self-reliant of the sons. He was also an exceptional marksman with a rifle. It was his job to see that he and his brothers and sisters got to school and back home safely. Daily, his alert blue eyes searched every dip and swell of the prairie for Indians. There had been occasions when the children of settlers were kidnapped by Native Americans and raised as one of their own. Bartholomew stood between his siblings and anyone seeking to do them harm. His vigilance and fearless attitude were qualities most needed to survive the times. His brothers and friends referred to him as a "chunk of steel."

Bartholomew never felt his name suited him. While he was still in school, he changed it to William Barclay and people close to him called him Bat. Bat didn't feel that farming suited him either.[7] He wanted to sample the adventure and excitement he'd read about in the numerous books he'd pored over. He was an avid reader who preferred books on the subject of sports and frontier travel. At the age of eighteen, he and his brother Ed left home and set a course for the southwestern part of Kansas. It was a location Bat believed was rich with opportunity.

During a stop over in Caldwell, the teenagers met several buffalo hunters. They were intrigued by the profession and were eager to learn all they could about the trade. Bat and Ed joined a buffalo hunting party and were hired on as skinners. It was backbreaking work, far removed from the romantic notion of Wild West living to which Bat had aspired. During the summer the stench from the rotting buffalo corpses was overpowering, and the flies were miles thick. In the winter it was next to impossible to keep your fingers warm and nimble long enough to separate the hide of the animal from the carcass. The Masterson brothers made lifelong friends with a number of the more than five thousand buffalo hunters and skinners plying their trade in the territory. Bat noted years later that it was "one of the only benefits of the grueling job."

In between hunting expeditions the Masterson boys followed the Atchison, Topeka, and Santa Fe Railroad to points between the Salt Fork on the Arkansas River and Colorado. Bustling prairie towns like Abilene lived up to every expectation Bat had about the untamed territory. The entrance to the saloons, dance halls, and gambling houses were like pearly gates to him. He liked to drink and play cards, and he was good at both. He was a shrewd judge of men and a bit of a mathematical genius as well.

The combination of the two made him an expert gambler. Bat wasn't interested in cards as a vocation, however. He felt he could more quickly secure a fortune by helping to push steel rail lines across the buffalo ranges.

In early May 1872, Bat and Ed signed on to work for Raymond Ritter, a subcontractor for the railroad. Ritter promised to pay the Mastersons and their friend Theo Raymond a substantial amount of money to level a five-mile section of land west of Fort Dodge toward the Colorado border. The three men finished the job in record time and were proudly watching as the first trains make their way down Dodge City's Front Street in September.

Bat and Ed had planned to use the wages they earned from the railroad work to invest in a business of their own. But by the time Bat went to collect their wages, Ritter had left the area. The brothers owed money to the businesses that supplied them with the material needed to do the grading, and they were determined to pay their debts. They returned to the buffalo ranges and raised enough funds to satisfy their bills. Bat's sense of right and wrong had been offended, and he vowed to catch Ritter in time and settle the score. There were few lawyers in Dodge, and Bat couldn't afford to hire one to exact justice anyway.

Bat could only afford a six-shooter, and after he purchased it, he waited patiently for Ritter's return. "One of these days he'll be pushing through here," he told Ed, "and I aim to be waiting at the station when he does."[8]

According to the diary of Josiah Wright Mooar, one of Bat's buffalo hunting friends, "Ritter returned to Dodge eight months after failing to honor his agreement with the Mastersons."[9] The news of his imminent arrival on the westbound train quickly reached Bat, and he hurried to the depot to confront the swindler. A crowd of Bat and Ed's associates quickly followed after him.

The vehicle had barely come to a stop when Bat boarded the passenger car. When he found Ritter, he calmly removed his gun from his holster, leveled it at the nervous man, and ordered him off the train.[10] Rumor had it that Ritter was in possession of more than three thousand dollars. "Peel $300 off that roll of money you're carrying," Bat told him, "or you'll never get back on that train alive." Ritter was outraged and scared and began shouting that he was being robbed and demanded that someone send for the sheriff. Nobody moved.

"They aren't going to bring the law," Bat assured him. "You're a crook, and I'm collecting a debt. Either you cough up, or you go back to Kansas City in a box."

Bat stared Ritter directly in the eye while pulling the hammer back on his gun. Ritter paid the determined young man what he owed, and Bat waved him back into the car. "Bat had not been noticed much before the incident," Mooar wrote, "but thereafter was considered a man to be reckoned with." Shortly after the event, Bat once more returned to the range to hunt buffalo. He joined an expedition headed for the heart of Indian territory in Texas. Native Americans were furious over the slaughter of the buffalo and the white man's encroachment onto their land and were willing to wage war to drive the white hunters out. Bat had survived the Prairie Indians aggressive behavior on more than one occasion while scouting buffalo stands on his own. His knowledge of their tactics, personal association with some of the warring braves, strength of character, and superior ability with a Sharps rifle made him a logical candidate for what promised to be a profitable outing.

The group of approximately twenty men saw no sign of Indians until they reached a trading post known as Adobe Walls, deep in the Texas Panhandle, where it was believed the buffalo would pass through. All the Southern Plains tribes had banded together to fight the white invaders and were keeping out of sight until just the right time. Bat and the others prepared for a battle they predicted would begin when the moon was full.

On June 26, 1874, a war party numbering in the hundreds attacked the small outpost and its inhabitants. Bat's stern blue eyes watched closely as the braves rode fast toward them, whooping and hollering. Bat and the other men took cover behind the thick walls of the buildings at the site. When the Indians came within range, members of the hunting party opened fire. "The red devils charged right down to the doors and portholes of the stockade," Bat later recalled, "but were met with withering fire from the cool brave men inside and had to retire time and time again. So close would they come that we planted our guns in their faces and against their bodies through the portholes, while they were raining their arrows and bullets down on us. For two terrible hours they made successive charges upon the walls, displaying a bravery and daring unsurpassed in any Indian battle."[11]

After five days of what would eventually be a two-week assault, Bat and a friend managed to slip away and ride to Fort Dodge for help. Bat's heroic actions at the Battle of Adobe Walls helped make him a renowned figure. The incident halted buffalo hunting for a time, and Bat drifted from jobs scouting for the cavalry and counting mules at a camp supply, to hiring on as a professional gambler in Deadwood, South Dakota, then to purchasing an interest in the Lone Star Dance Hall in Dodge City.

Bat not only distinguished himself from other men with his talent for a variety of vocations, but also in the way he dressed. Residents of Dodge said he was the "best dressed man in town." Bat wore gold mounted spurs, a crimson Mexican sash around his waist, a red silk neckerchief, a bowler hat, and ivory-handled revolvers.

Bat was one of Dodge City's most admired and successful business owners. With few exceptions he got along well with everyone and gratefully benefited from the numerous cowboys that frequented his saloon. Although he disapproved of the violent actions the cattlemen indulged in when they returned from a drive, he was opposed to the city officials' desire to overly regulate their behavior. Together with other prosperous business owners, Bat supported a wide-open policy that gave rowdy cowhands free reign over the town. Wealthy residents such as James Kelley and Bob Wright, along with many rough frontier men, formed an organization called the Dodge City Gang to champion their liberal position. Bat frequently spoke out in favor of the "Gang" and its attempts to maintain the wild character of the town.

A group of equally powerful men, professing to stand for law and order, fought against the gang. They used their political influence to pass ordinances to deal with the over-the-top actions of the cattlemen. Town leaders appointed George Hoover mayor of Dodge, and Hoover quickly hired a team of police officers to enforce the new laws, one of which barred firearms within the city limits.

Bat believed Mayor Hoover and Larry Deger, the overweight saloon keeper he named as marshal, were abusing the power they had been given and were behaving more like bullies than public servants. Marshal Deger and some of his deputies arrested, and many times assaulted, anyone deemed mildly annoying. The harsh treatment toward the cowboys upset Bat's sense of fair play. On June 6, 1877, he tried to prevent officials from bringing in a harmless braggart who'd had too much to drink. An article in the *Dodge City Times* described the incident.

"Last Wednesday was a lively day for Dodge. Two hundred cattlemen in the city; the gang in good shape for business; merchants happy, and money flooding the city, is a condition of affairs that could continue in Dodge very long without an eruption, and that is the way it was last Wednesday. Robert Gilmore was making a talk for himself in a rather emphatic manner to which Marshal Deger took exception and started for the dog house with him. Bobby walked very leisurely, so much so that Larry felt it necessary to administer a few paternal kicks in the rear. This act was soon interrupted by Bat Masterson, who wound his arm affectionately around the Marshal's neck and let the prisoner escape. Deger then grappled with Bat, at the same time calling upon the bystanders to take the offender's gun and assist in the arrest. Bat Masterson would not surrender yet, and came near getting hold of a pistol from among several which were strewn around over the sidewalk, but half a dozen Texas men came to the Marshal's aid and gave him a chance to draw his gun and beat Bat over the head until blood flew upon Joe Mason so that he kicked, and warded off the blows with his arm. Bat Masterson seemed possessed of extraordinary strength, and every inch of the way was closely contested, but the city dungeon was reached at last, and in he went. If he had got hold of his gun before going in, there would have been a general killing."[12]

With the exception of Bat's brothers, Ed and James (James followed his siblings to Dodge in early 1876), and Wyatt Earp, who served as assistants or deputies under Larry Deger, Bat believed Deger's administration was corrupt and ineffective. Wyatt challenged Bat to do something about it and take Deger on in the upcoming election for sheriff. "I never had a hankering for being a lawman," Bat told Wyatt. "It just means more shooting." "Then what are those guns doing on your hip?" Wyatt asked. "How will I handle rough customers I see walking around me with a game leg?"

Bat pointed out. "You aren't going to kick 'em into the jail-house," Wyatt told him.[13]

Shortly after Bat expressed an interest in law enforcement, Sheriff Charlie Bassett appointed him as under sheriff. Bat was tough, but fair, and was usually able to head off trouble before it started. He treated the cattlemen who brought prosperity to Dodge hospitably. Bat eagerly campaigned for the job of sheriff making no promises, admitting to voters that he was no politician. He told them he would do his best to handle the office properly and with dignity. On November 6, 1877, he was elected sheriff. When he took over the job in January 1878, he immediately named Charlie Bassett as his under sheriff.

Bat had the temperament for work as a policeman. He was confident in his own skills. He had reservations about his brother Ed's abilities however. Ed was diligent, but he had too gentle a disposition for a lawman. Bat tried to persuade his brother to leave law enforcement, but to no avail.

On the night of April 9, 1878, Bat's worst fears were realized. Marshal Ed and his deputy rushed to the Lady Gay Dance Hall to investigate shots that had been fired. They found six rowdy cowboys making a public nuisance of themselves. Ed Masterson noted that John Wagner was carrying a revolver contrary to city ordinance, so he asked him to hand it over. Wagner gave the gun to the marshal who turned it over to Wagner's boss, A. M. Walker, advising him to check it with the bartender. Ed and the deputy then stepped outside. Within a short time Wagner came out, and Ed could see that he was wearing a shoulder gun.

"Give me that gun, Wagner!" commanded Marshal Masterson. "To hell with you," Wagner spat back. A shot sounded, and Ed Masterson slumped to the boardwalk with a bullet through his abdomen. The marshal staggered into Hoover's Saloon and told George Hinkle, "George, I'm shot," then collapsed unconscious.

Hinkle put out a fire in Ed's clothes that had been caused by the close-range shot, apparently fired by Wagner. Ed was carried to Bat's room, where he died an hour later without having regained consciousness. Bat and a handful of other police officers rushed to the scene. Walker and Wagner drifted with the crowd to the Peacock Saloon. Suddenly shots rang out; both Wagner and Walker were wounded. Wagner staggered into the Peacock Saloon, falling in a heap at the feet of the saloon's owner, Ham Bell. He died the next morning. Walker had been seriously wounded.

Bat buried Ed at the Fort Dodge Cemetery and returned to work a few days later, but his life was never the same. He blamed himself for not looking after Ed better. His position on gun control changed radically after the shooting. He was determined that no one who wasn't a lawman would be allowed to brandish a weapon in Dodge City. The men involved in Ed Masterson's shooting were arrested, but later released because the judge could not determine positively they had a hand in it. The blatant injustice of the situation sparked a general distrust of the legal system in Bat, and if not for the influence of friends like Bill Tilghman, he could be driven to disregard the law and deal with outlaws on his own terms.[14]

As the rain and hail cascaded down around the small section of earth Bat and the other posse members occupied, he reflected on Ed's senseless death and how he wanted to handle Dora Hand's killer for committing the same kind of random act. He felt the same dogged responsibility for Dora's murder that he did for Ed's. It drove him.

A thousand plans, all wild and disjointed, ran through his brain as dawn neared. As if the men in the posse each sensed it was time to move on, they rose to their feet and began loading their gear onto their horses. The haggard, sleep-deprived group mounted their rides and slowly inched their way along the creek. The sky cleared just before sunrise, and each of the men surveyed the muddy ground more closely searching for naked hoof prints. But any serious hope the lawmen had of finding James Kenedy's trail had been washed away in the rain.

They stopped and dismounted when they were within a mile of the safest and easiest spot to cross on the Cimarron River. The river was overflowing its banks and the current was fierce. "He couldn't have crossed the river last night," Charlie said matter-of-factly. "The rain would have kept him from doing that." "We'll find him," Bill assured the others as he walked his mount over the soggy soil.[15]

Wyatt and Charlie followed after Bill, carefully drinking in the immediate surroundings, looking for signs of Dora's murderer. Bat brought up the rear wrestling with the notion that James Kenedy might really be halfway to Cheyenne. He slowly pushed the thought out of his head.

CHAPTER SIX

BEYOND THE RIVER

They have gone in search of the fellows who commit-
ted the deed . . . but I am afraid the trouble has not
ended, as some twenty of the Texas men went out after
the officers.

FANNIE GARRETTSON WRITING
FROM DODGE CITY, OCTOBER 5, 1878

F og and a heavy morning mist danced across the wet
scrub and brush grass that stretched toward the sun.
The posse rode through the somewhat eerie scene without
speaking, their faces a study of relentless purpose, their
senses alive and straining. Their keen eyes searched for vegetation that had been trampled, twigs that had been broken,
ground that been packed down, remnants of clothing, any
sign that a desperate rider had passed through the area.

Wyatt Earp leaned slightly out of his saddle to study the
terrain and the crude path they were following. His expression was resolute. He sniffed at the wind that began to rise
and coaxed his horse into a trot beside Charlie Bassett and
Bill Tilghman's roans. The men rode three abreast spurred
on by an unspoken belief that they were headed in the right
direction.

Bat Masterson lingered behind the others, glancing back
over his shoulder at someone he felt was following them.

Wyatt caught a glimpse of Bat bringing up the rear, pulled back on the reins of his mount, turned the animal around, and rode toward the lawman. "Bat," Wyatt said, scanning the surroundings cautiously. Bat smiled at Wyatt, but behind the smile was a look of uneasiness. "Remember when we were hunting buffalo?" Bat asked. Wyatt nodded. "We'd find a spot upwind of them and pick them off one by one," Bat continued. "They never even stampeded when members of their herd began dropping. Not so long as they didn't get a whiff of the hunter. All we had to do was make sure we stayed out of smelling range and drop each animal with one shot." Wyatt peered warily into the distance they'd traveled. The significance of Bat's memory resonated in his head. Bat walked his horse past Wyatt's animal. "All we had to do was stay out of smelling range," he repeated as he rode by. Wyatt gave another guarded look over the countryside then fell in after Bat.[1]

In the two years Wyatt and Bat had served together as lawmen in Ford County, they'd had numerous run-ins with rowdy Texas cowhands. Both men knew any of those vengeful drovers and their crew could be just out of sight waiting to gun them down.

There were most assuredly rogue Indian braves, either Cheyenne or Comanche, keeping a watchful eye on the posse, but the policemen didn't believe they were a threat. The bulk of the Plains Indians had been confined to reservations and generally would not launch an attack unless provoked. If there was anyone lurking beyond the tall grasses and iodine bushes, anyone following the lawmen using the crevices in the earth for cover, it was presumed to be the cowpunchers from the Kenedy family ranch. "They're on their way," Bat said, referring to James Kenedy's fellow drovers.

After eight years in law enforcement, Wyatt Earp knew the risks and sacrifices that came with keeping the peace. Many of his friends and acquaintances insisted he was born for the job. One of the men who hunted buffalo with Wyatt recalled that he had "absolute confidence in himself that gave him an edge over the run of men." Bat Masterson regarded him as someone who was "absolutely destitute of physical fear."[2]

Wyatt Earp was born on March 19, 1848, the same year gold was discovered and hordes of immigrants rushed to California. His father, Nicholas, would eventually move his wife and children to the Gold Country, but only after their peaceful family life had been disrupted by the Civil War.

Raised primarily on a farm in Pella, Iowa, Wyatt worked the homestead plowing and hoeing alongside his five brothers and three sisters. According to Wyatt, his father instilled in the Earp children a "regard for the land that was equaled by his respect for the law and his detestation for lawless elements so prevalent in the West."[3]

At the age of thirteen, Wyatt left home with the desire to join the army and fight for the Union. His older brothers were already serving, and he wanted to be a part of the fight. His father stopped him from enlisting and brought him home. Before the war ended, Nicholas had moved his brood, including his permanently wounded soldier-son James, to Southern California. Wyatt grew up fast on the trail to San Bernadino

County. His father's age and brother's injury forced him to assume a large responsibility for the more than forty wagons making the journey together. He hunted game for the travelers with a combination rifle-shotgun weapon that James taught him to use, and competently helped defend them against Indian raiding parties.

Once they reached their destination, the Earp family resumed their farming ventures at the new location, but Wyatt was wholly unsatisfied with the work. Anxious to strike out on his own and possessed with an adventurous spirit, he defied his father and left home.

He teamed up with his brother Virgil, who by this time had completed his term in the service and was employed as a freight runner. The pair hauled goods back and forth from California to Salt Lake City. After awhile Wyatt grew tired of that work and hired on as a grader with the Union Pacific Railroad. He traveled the wild frontier for four years with no particular aspiration apart from frequenting rough railroad construction camps.

In 1868 Wyatt's parents and younger siblings moved back to the Midwest and settled in the small town of Lamar, Missouri. Twenty-year-old Wyatt wasn't far behind. He reluctantly tried his hand at farming again before accepting an appointment as constable. Lamar was a quiet community with few actual lawbreakers. With the exception of arresting an occasional drunk and disorderly character and herding stray hogs off the street, there was little to do in the way of law enforcement.

On January 3, 1870, Wyatt married Urilla Sutherland. Less than a year later, she died. The cause of her death was unclear. The loss and subsequent squabble between Wyatt and his late wife's brothers over Urilla's death left the lawman despondent and adrift.

His sad circumstances were made worse by a false allegation of fraud. Shortly after his wife died, a prominent citizen accused Wyatt of falsifying the amount he paid the constable and his bondsmen to carry out a sentence. The case was brought to court and later dismissed. Wyatt left the area soon after and headed to Oklahoma.

The territory was lacking in civility. Indians threatened by whites encroaching on their homeland were fighting back against the invaders. Rustlers and horse thieves terrorized homesteaders. Thunderstorms, deadly cold winters, floods, and scorching summers added to the unrest of the area. Wyatt quickly made his presence felt in the already volatile region. Still nursing a broken heart and bitter over the recent fracas in Missouri, he quickly found himself in the center of another controversy. This time he was accused of stealing horses. A witness claimed that he and another man absconded with a pair of stallions. Wyatt was indicted and set to stand trial, but the matter was dismissed from court after his alleged accomplice was acquitted in a separate trial.

On the move again, Wyatt hired out his expertise with a gun to the government and provided game for surveying crews measuring land boundaries in Oklahoma, Missouri, and Kansas. He wandered in and out of settlements and tent cities across the midsection of the country visiting saloons where boxing matches were held and honing his gambling skills.

Bat Masterson knew Wyatt to be a fine faro player and a man who did not tolerate any insinuation that he ran a crooked game. At a saloon in Gunnison, Colorado, where Wyatt had set up a faro table, a local, dishonest character named Ike Morris publicly accused Wyatt and his dealer of cheating. The scene Ike made was meant to drive the trade from Wyatt's game to his own and force his competitor to leave town.

Wyatt investigated the claim and learned that his dealer had indeed cheated Morris. The crowd that gathered at the saloon waited with bated breath to see how the situation would unfold. "The dealer wronged you," Wyatt told Morris, "and I'd like to return your money on that account." Morris grinned big. "But," Wyatt added, "you are looked upon in this part of the country as a bad man, and if I give you back your money you would say as soon as I left, that you made me do it, and for that reason I will keep the money." The long silence following Wyatt's statement was painful for Morris to endure. His grin faded, but Wyatt maintained a serious, no-nonsense expression. Morris said nothing more about the matter and within a couple of days of the incident left the area.

Wyatt eventually headed back to the Plains states where young men with no prospects for employment were assembling to hunt buffalo. Expert shots like Wyatt, Bat Masterson, and Bat's brother, Ed, who Earp had met on the range in Kansas in 1871, could kill and skin twenty to twenty-five buffalo a day. The profit was substantial. "I went into the business to make money," Wyatt admitted about the trade, "while enjoying a life that appealed to me."

Wyatt's stint as a buffalo hunter led him to the raw, unruly cattle town of Ellsworth, Kansas. His reputation as a daring and reckless man preceded him. In less than a month after his arrival in August 1873, he was asked to pin a badge on and disarm a gunman who had killed a sheriff.

Texas gunman Ben Thompson and his brother Billy were drinking and gambling at the Brennan's Saloon when a poker game went awry, heated words were exchanged, and bullets flew. The result was the shooting death of one of Ellsworth's most popular lawmen, Happy Jack. The men responsible for the shooting were ordered by the town mayor to surrender their weapons, but they refused. The Thompsons' position was backed by a crowd of Texas cowhands armed and ready to fight. The mayor dismissed the entire police force for not challenging the lawbreakers and arresting them. Billy Thompson made a fast getaway. With no one left to diffuse the explosive situation, the mayor turned to the one man many believed would not be afraid to handle the delicate matter, Wyatt Earp.

After quickly being appointed city marshal, Wyatt boldly approached Ben in the street and advised him to throw down his gun or be killed.[4] "I thought he would shoot me," Wyatt later recalled. "I really expected to be killed unless I could see his wrist move in time to draw and fire before he would pull the trigger . . . I just kept looking him in the eye as I walked toward him. And when he started talking to me, I was pretty sure I had him. I tried to talk in as pleasant a voice as I could manage, and I told him to throw his gun in the road. He did and that's all there was to it."[5]

Wyatt escorted Ben Thompson to jail and news of the quiet way he took care of the desperate gunfighter spread to other rough-and-tumble burgs throughout Kansas. Public officials in Wichita hired the part-time lawman to bring order to their town in 1874. While serving on the police force, he tracked down drovers who had skipped out on debts owed to local business owners, kept the peace between drunken cowhands, collected taxes, and investigated a few murders.

More often than not, Wyatt was able to subdue outlaws without ever pulling his gun. He was naturally good with his fists and having observed fighters in numerous boxing matches had become a cunning pugilist in his own right.[6]

Bat Masterson claimed that Wyatt "never, at any time in his career, resorted to the pistol excepting in cases where such a course was absolutely necessary. Wyatt could scrap with his fist, and had often taken all the fight out of bad men, as they were called, with no other weapons than those provided by nature." [7] If offenders could not be brought down with a punch or two, he used the butt of his gun. A hard rap on the skull with the end of a six-shooter rendered many out-of-control men unconscious.

When Wyatt wasn't doing police work, he was dealing cards at gambling houses and keno parlors. Although he kept company with people who liked to drink, he did not partake himself. "In all the years during which I was intimately associated with Wyatt, as a buffalo hunter and a peace officer," Bill Tilghman told his wife, "I never knew him to take a drink of liquor."[8] Abstaining from alcohol gave Wyatt a further advantage over gun-wielding opponents.

Many Texas cattlemen who had driven their herds to Wichita and then celebrated by getting drunk and shooting up the town had confrontations with Wyatt. They resented his nerve and the way he enforced the law. In fact, cattlemen held a grudge against him that followed the legend to his next job. He didn't get along too well with other lawmen either. A disagreement between Wyatt and a fellow police officer led to his leaving Wichita. After beating the man to a pulp for insulting the town marshal, Wyatt was fined and fired from the force. Disgusted by the decision, he rode on to the most dangerous cow town in Kansas, Dodge City.

Once a drunken cowboy got on a train bound for Kansas. He had no ticket, but he held a wad of money in his hand. When the conductor took his money and asked the cowboy where he wanted to go the cowboy said, "Straight to hell." Without blinking the conductor said, "All right, that will be one ticket straight to Dodge City." Wyatt had frequented many tough towns whose life blood was cattle and was mainly populated by wild ranch hands, prostitutes, and railroad workers, but Dodge was every bit as delinquent as people said it was.

Wyatt arrived in town in April 1876. His arrival did not escape the attention of city officials on the lookout for men with nerve enough to wear a badge and keep the wild elements that lived there in check. Wyatt was offered the job of assistant marshal. Serving on a combined force with the Ford County's sheriff's office, he took his place alongside the most formidable lawmen in the West. Earp's salary was $250 a month and he earned an additional $2.50 for every arrest he made.

Like the other officers, he was hired to cut down on the gunplay in Dodge.

He was firm with rowdy drovers who took their good times to extreme, but he was also conscious of their economic impact on the community. "I figured that if the cowboys were manhandled and heaved into the calaboose every time they showed in town with guns on, or out loose in the forbidden territory," Wyatt confessed, "they'd come to time quicker than if we kept them primed for gunplay."[9]

In September 1876, Wyatt had had his fill of battling with cowboys.

He left Dodge, and he and his brother Morgan made their way to Deadwood, South Dakota. After earning a considerable amount selling firewood to camp settlers and prospectors, they hired on as guards for a freighter service transporting gold ore. By spring the following year, Wyatt was back in Kansas and back at work as an assistant in Dodge City.

Wyatt proved to be an exceptional policeman racking up more than three hundred arrests in a month's time. The May 14, 1877, edition of the *Ford County Globe* called Earp "the most efficient officer Dodge ever had." He disarmed many cowhands, teamsters, and hunters and helped bring about a more congenial atmosphere, but the way he enforced the law infuriated Texans, as it had in Wichita. Lawbreaking cattlemen found it insulting to be stripped of their weapons (which were illegal to carry in town) and beaten unconscious before being taken to jail. They believed Wyatt and his cohorts should make their stand with a pistol or at least a knife.

Given Wyatt's ability with a six-shooter there were those who were content with the deputy not using his gun. On July 21, 1877, the *Dodge City Times* warned gunslingers against drawing on Wyatt unless they "got the drop and meant to burn powder without any preliminary talk."

The officers that served Ford County and Dodge City were an extraordinary force. Strong and dedicated men like Joe Mason, Neal Brown, Jim Masterson, and William Duffy protected the region along with Wyatt and the other well-known members of the "intrepid posse." All were effective in their own right, but it was Bat and Wyatt who got the most attention. The pair often tackled troublemakers together. They strategically placed shotguns about the town in order to protect themselves from groups of armed offenders hoping to overtake them. They subdued wanted criminals as peacefully as they could, backing each other's play no matter how dangerous the circumstance.

Newspaper articles praising the job Wyatt and his cohorts were doing further fueled the hatred many cattlemen had for him. In the summer of 1878, an attempt was made to collect a $1,000 bounty offered by unknown influential and irate Texans to kill Wyatt Earp.

On the evening of July 26, Wyatt was making the usual rounds and had stopped momentarily outside the door of the Comique Theatre where comedian Eddie Foy was entertaining a packed house. Wyatt noticed a cowboy pass by on his horse, turn around at the end of the street, and then repeat the process. On the second pass he quickly turned his horse around and spurred the animal into a full gallop. He fired a volley of shots at the lawman as he rode by. Wyatt drew on the shooter knocking him out of his saddle with the second shot, which proved to be fatal. Bat Masterson, who was inside the theater at the time of the incident, rushed to Wyatt's aid and exchanged fire with a few cowboys that had joined in the ruckus.[10]

The gunman Wyatt hit was identified as a Texan by the name of George Hoy. There was a warrant out for his arrest for criminal acts committed in Texas. Before dying from the bullet wound, George confessed that a wealthy cattleman had promised to take care of his legal troubles if he killed Wyatt. He refused to say who the cattleman was.

News of George's passing appeared in the August 27, 1878, edition of the *Ford County Globe*. The report made it clear that he was well liked and had several associates who looked after him. "George was apparently rather a good man," the article stated, "having those chivalrous qualities, so common to frontiersmen, well developed . . . He had many friends and no enemies among Texas men who knew him. George was nothing but a poor cowboy, but his brother cowboys permitted him to want for nothing during his illness, and buried him in grand style when dead, which was very creditable to them. We have been informed by those who pretended to know that the deceased, although under bond for a misdemeanor in Texas, was in no wise a criminal, and would have been released at the next setting of the court if he had not been removed by death from its jurisdiction."

Tension between the Texas cowboys and Wyatt, Bat, and law enforcement in Dodge City as a whole were at a near breaking point by the time James Kenedy rode into town and shot Dora Hand. Drovers aching to get even for what they believed was an "abuse of power" plotted to finish the job George Hoy started. Wyatt and the other members of the posse were aware of the vendetta and ready for whatever trouble they might be riding into.

By late afternoon of the second day of the hunt for James Kenedy, the posse was exhausted and so were their mounts. They were confident the man they were after hadn't left

Kansas, but they hadn't come across any significant sign that Kenedy was in the vicinity.

They rode steadily along, their clothes stiff with dried mud, their hair matted, and dirt caked into the creases of their faces. They hurried their pace only after the outline of a crude ranch house standing alone in the vast flatland came into view.

The house was made of sod, solidly built, with a cross-timbered roof and deep windows. A small, inviting porch extended across the front of the building and smoke curled out of a chimney and hovered over a nearby corral. A dog barked excitedly as the horsemen slowly rode toward the house and dismounted. Just as the men stepped onto the porch, the owner of the homestead opened the front door slightly and peered out. Bat introduced the posse and himself to the man and pushed the lapel back on his duster to show the badge hanging off his vest. After studying the lawmen for a moment, the apprehensive rancher inched the door open a little farther. "You're a long way from Dodge, ain't you?" he asked. "We're looking for a man," Bat told him flatly. "And you trailed him here?" the man inquired curiously. "Have you seen anyone passing through?" Bill pressed in a kind, but firm tone. The rancher nodded. "Yesterday," he replied, "before the storm . . . and he seemed in a hurry too."[11]

Bat glanced over at the posse's worn-out rides and carefully considered the next course of action.

"We're going to hold up here for a bit," he informed the homesteader. "Help yourself," the man said. Charlie and Wyatt returned to the horses and removed the saddles from the backs of their weary animals. Bat and Bill stood guard, eyeing the surroundings for anything that moved. Darkness slowly crept over the cattle farm and somewhere off in the near distance a coyote yapped. The rancher stepped out of his house and motioned for the men to come inside and eat.

A light rain began to fall as the men sauntered toward the house. "We've got a chance to pick up his trail at dawn," Bill told his fellow riders. Frustrated, Bat stared up at the thunderclouds and let the rain wash over his face. "A damn slim one if you ask me," he snapped.

CHAPTER SEVEN

WAITING FOR A KILLER

Four pistol shots awakened the echoes in that dull misty morning, and aroused the police force and others. Pistol shots are of common occurrence, but this firing betokened something fatal.

DODGE CITY TIMES ARTICLE ABOUT
THE MURDER OF DORA HAND, OCTOBER 12, 1878

A cold morning broke in rose-and-gold colors over the vast Cimarron grassland. James Kenedy tumbled out of his rocky bed tucked under a long, narrow mesa and rubbed the sleep out of his eyes. He hauled his weary frame to a depression in the earth; turned his back to the frigid, biting wind; and began relieving himself. His tired horse meandered behind him, alternating between gnawing on bits of brush and drinking from deep puddles made by the rain that had assaulted the region.

James finished his business and dragged himself to the saddle and bit he had removed from his mount the night before. The horse gave the outlaw a disapproving look as he approached with the harness. Dried lather from profuse sweating had beaded up across the animal's backside, and his unshod hooves were tender and chipped.

The idea of riding on wasn't any more appealing to James than to his horse, but it was necessary. The downpour

Dora was a performer at the Comique and Variety Theatres in Dodge City. She was known as a "prepossessing woman and artful, winning ways brought many admirers within her smiles and blandishments."
Courtesy of Kansas Heritage Center, Dodge City

The Long Branch Saloon was one of the most popular taverns in Dodge City. Lawmen and outlaws alike spent time at the saloon.
Courtesy of Kansas Heritage Center, Dodge City

James Kenedy ran to the Long Branch Saloon shortly after firing his gun at Mayor Kelley's house.
Courtesy of Kansas Heritage Center, Dodge City

Fannie Garrettson—in a period cutout—was a friend and roommate of Dora Hand at the time of her death—1878.
Courtesy of Kansas Heritage Center, Dodge City

On their way to becoming famous lawmen, Wyatt Earp,
Bill Tilghman, Charlie Bassett, and Bat Masterson hunted buffalo
along the rail lines.
Courtesy of the Library of Congress

Fort Dodge was one of the most important forts on the western
frontier. Dodge City's mayor James Kelley was a patient at the
hospital there the night Dora Hand was shot and killed.
Courtesy of the Kansas State Historical Society

Mayor James Kelley posed with a few of his prized greyhound dogs.
Courtesy of the Kansas State Historical Society

Thousands of head of cattle were driven down the main thoroughfare of Dodge throughout the mid- to late 1800s. Mayor James Kelley's saloon, Beatty and Kelley, is in the foreground of the photograph.
Courtesy of Kansas Heritage Center, Dodge City

*The "intrepid posse" and James Kenedy traveled this section
of the Kansas terrain on their way toward the Cimarron River.*
Courtesy of the Library of Congress

This group gunfighter shot was taken in 1871 in Dodge City.
Top row, left to right: W. H. Harris, Luke Short, Bat Masterson,
and W. F. Petillon. Bottom row, left to right: Charlie Bassett,
Wyatt Earp, Frank McLain, and Neal Brown.
Courtesy of Kansas Heritage Center, Dodge City

Bat earned his nickname,
in part, by hitting offenders over
the head with his silver-
handled walking stick.
His name was synonymous
with both bravery and nerve.
Courtesy of Kansas Heritage
Center, Dodge City

Bill Tilghman was a deputy sheriff in Ford County from 1884 to 1886 and the marshal of Dodge City during the same time. He was dedicated to bringing the law to a land where there was none.
Courtesy of Kansas Heritage Center, Dodge City

Wyatt Earp, shown here in his middle years, served as an assistant marshal of Dodge City and became a deacon of Dodge City's Union Church.
Courtesy of Kansas Heritage Center, Dodge City

from the previous evening had no doubt raised the level of the river, but James was hopeful that the water had crested and would begin receding by late afternoon.[1] If that happened, the ford would be passable and James and the cowboys he was sure his father had sent after him, could make it across.

No matter what trouble James had ever managed to get himself into, he knew there was sanctuary in Texas. His father had recently purchased Laureles Ranch, a 130,000-acre spread twenty miles from Corpus Christi, and had hired a team of ranch hands to fence in the property. Mifflin Kenedy planned to build up his herds, raise a better quality of livestock, and isolate his rebellious son from persistent police or vengeful gunslingers.[2]

For a brief moment in time, Mifflin had believed his spoiled boy had a future with the Texas Rangers. In November 1875 James joined a company whose main objective was to reduce the raids on cattle ranches by Mexican bandits.[3] His knowledge of the wild territory made him a valuable asset to the troops, but his term of duty lasted only five months. In April 1876 he voluntarily left the Rangers earning a mere $59.72 for his time served.

Law and order was not in James's nature. He thrived on misdeeds and violent confrontations with competing ranchers outside of the Texas Panhandle. He relished every kind of indulgence and came and went his own sweet way. He could not conceive of a single circumstance where he would not ultimately be rescued from the consequences of his vicious actions.

He swaggered back to his flimsy bedroll under the mesa and bent down to gather the rest of his gear. Suddenly his eyes went wide with alarm, and his hand flashed toward the six-shooter strapped to his side. A rattlesnake lay not two feet from his saddlebag and shotgun—its protective covering blending in with the ground. The early morning fall sun didn't provide enough warmth to drive the torpor out of the snake, but it was beginning to lift its head, and its tongue was darting. It was coiled and James didn't know how long it was. His draw was fast and fluid. He fired without apparent aim, and the bullet tore through the S-shaped coils.

James wiped the back of his hand across his forehead and there was shakiness in the gesture. He turned on his heels and with his gun still drawn, quickly gave the area around him a once-over. In retrospect he wished he'd never fired his weapon. It was instinct, but it might have drawn unwanted attention.

With no regard for his horse's condition, he quickly cinched the saddle tightly on the animal's back, sunk his boots into the stirrup, and threw himself on the ride. With staggering self-assurance James led the horse away from the scant hideout onto the plains.

In the meantime, according to an account in the October 12, 1878, edition of the *Dodge City Times,* Bill and Bat sat hunkered down behind a cluster of boulders several hundred yards from the sod ranch house. Bat eyed the horizon—strain and tension showed in every line of his face. Bill carefully examined the view as well. His eyes were just as bloodshot as

Bat's. Nothing was moving. It was calm, tranquil. "Thought I heard something a bit ago," Bat said in a tone that was flat and unemotional. "Guess it was just wishful thinking," he concluded. Bill knew that Bat continued to wrestle with the notion that James Kenedy would ride boldly past them to get to the ford. Bat knew the desperado was arrogant, but he also knew that criminals could be unpredictable.

In early 1878, Sheriff Masterson had assembled a posse to track down members of the Rourke-Rudabaugh Gang, outlaws who had held up the Santa Fe train. The February 5, 1878, edition of the *Ford County Globe* boasted that Bat and his men had "the sand and nerve to go where no other men on earth dares to go. If the robbers are not captured, it will not be for want of bravery, coolness or strategy."

Bat and his posse trailed the thieves in the dark to the banks of the Cimarron River. They rode for more than twenty-four hours straight to catch the train robbers, but lost them when the outlaws took an unexpected turn off the anticipated route. Bat was discouraged with the outcome and frustrated with himself for not better anticipating the gang's next move. Although he did eventually capture four of the gang members including Dave Rudabaugh, their notorious leader, Bat was determined to never repeat his mistake.[4] He respected the men with whom he now rode and their experience and for those reasons he yielded to their judgment.

As sure as Bill was that the posse had the advantage on Kenedy, he'd also seen his share of manhunts that had gone bad. The initial search for a horse thief named George Snyder ended with the criminal disappearing into an area of the Panhandle near Oklahoma that had no government or legal status and was a refuge for thieves and murderers.[5] Bill was determined to apprehend the outlaw no matter where he was hiding.

Before riding 350 miles to Mobeetie, Texas, Snyder's rumored location, Bill acquired the necessary warrants to bring him back to Dodge. Most law enforcement officers wouldn't have bothered to get extradition papers from the governor of Kansas, then present them to the governor of Texas prior to going after the offender. George Snyder didn't expect Bill to go to the effort either. He assumed he wasn't in any danger of being arrested inside the borders of Texas.

Bill found George at a saloon. The horse thief was engrossed in a poker game when the deputy walked up behind him. "Snyder," Bill addressed the man, "I'm a law officer. You're wanted back in Dodge." Stunned, George turned around and faced Bill. Bill's hand was poised over his gun, ready to act if the man made a false move. "You can't arrest me!" George announced. "This is Texas!" "And the Governor has honored a requisition for you," Bill replied coolly. "So you better put up your hands and come along."[6]

George thought for a moment, then dived under the table and quickly crawled out the other side. Bill didn't bother with ducking in after him. Instead, he stepped onto the table, scattering poker chips and cards all over the floor. He grabbed George's ankle and jerked him down to the ground. The crook's arms were flaying as he continued to fight off the arrest. Bill found the man's jaw with his fist and knocked him out.

The Mobeetie marshal entered just as the skirmish was coming to an end and demanded to know what was going on. After explaining the situation, Bill presented him with the extradition papers. The marshal reviewed the documents, looked down at George, and then turned back to Bill with a puzzled look on his face. "You went to a lot trouble," he said, giving the papers another read. "If he stole the horse, why didn't you just shoot him?"

Bat continued to scrutinize the terrain around him. A pair of pheasant nearby leaped into the air with sudden flurry. The two men watched them land then take off again. Bat shot Bill an impatient look and Bill almost smiled. "At least it ain't raining," he said.

Charlie patted his saddle-worn horse on the neck, slid his hand down the animal's leg, and curled his hoof up so he could inspect it. Mud and debris from the hard ride had accumulated between the hoof and the shoe and he gently began scraping it out with a knife. Wyatt was close by scouting the surrounding plains with a pair of binoculars. His mount stood beside him munching on vegetation underfoot. "We need to turn these horses further out to graze," Charlie said finishing with his ride's last shoe. "Put some distance between ourselves and the ranch. There can't be any signs of a sheriff's posse," he added. Wyatt nodded and slapped his horse on the rear, and the animal trotted a little ways away from him.[7]

Charlie coaxed his ride off as well then walked over to Bat's and Bill's horses huddled in the same area eating and nudged them apart. Frustrated by the interruption, the mounts launched into a short run and settled some distance from the men.

"Did you ever meet Mifflin Kenedy?" Charlie asked Wyatt. "No," Wyatt replied unconcerned. "I've just heard about him." "He's a man who will back his boy's play no matter how low his character is," Charlie noted. "That's what I've heard," Wyatt responded.

A couple of years prior to the posse's ride after James, Charlie had met a father with the same dedication Mifflin had for his child. The difference was his son hadn't done anything wrong. The event was fresh in the lawman's mind as he sat staring out over the plains. The father's name was R. C. Calleham and he was a sewing machine salesman from Topeka.[8] His son was a cowhand who had a camp fifteen miles from Dodge City on Saw Log Creek. A horse thief by the name of Cole rode into John's camp one evening, and John invited him to share the spot with him. John didn't know Cole was a horse thief with a vigilante group fast on his trail. When the group caught up with the thief, they assumed John was his accomplice and hanged them both on the spot.

Charlie was the sheriff of Ford County at the time he received a letter from John's father, R. C., about the matter. The letter had also been signed by the governor of Kansas encouraging the sheriff to investigate the "facts and circumstances attending the death of my son." Calleham maintained that his son was "innocent" and noted that "his lynching demanded the attention of all law-abiding people, and more especially of the officers to whom is entrusted the execution of the law and the preservation of the public peace." At the same time, the governor asked the sheriff to put an end to the mob violence and bring justice to the perpetrators.

Charlie didn't know much about the case, but after looking into the matter, learned that there was validity in R. C. Calleham's claims. He sent word back to Governor Thomas Osborn explaining his findings and what he needed to do to resolve the situation. "Through what little information I gave him and his own exertions," Charlie wrote, "Mr. Calleham has asserted that his son was at Dodge City on the 3rd day of April 1876, the day on which we held our municipal election. It appears from the statements made by the Sumner County and other papers that the horses were stolen on the 30th inst., and that the parties in pursuit followed the thieves a distance of 300 miles. The theory is that if the deceased, John Calleham, was here on the 3rd day of April that it would be physically impossible for him to have stolen those horses. Several citizens of good standing are willing to qualify that they spoke with him on the 3rd day of April, at Dodge City. If he was one of the thieves, the time given him to travel over 300 miles of ground was 3 days from the night of the 30th of March to the morning of the 3rd of April. I do not hesitate to say that the feat could not be performed by any one horse or horseman in the time given, especially as the ground was so soft as to leave an impression, so plain that it could be followed at a very rapid gait. To be brief I am now of the opinion that the man was innocent of the crime alleged, and for which he has suffered death." [9]

Charlie concluded his letter by explaining that his office lacked the necessary funds to hire the additional officers to arrest the people involved in the hanging or to make the lengthy journey to find them. He further felt it would not be wise to inform the Sumner County sheriff because he believed he would tip off the lynch mob, and they would escape.

The governor's reply was quick and to the point. Although he was anxious for the parties who executed Calleham to be brought to justice, there were no public funds from which to draw. Officially, there was nothing else Charlie could do.

The situation never set well with Charlie. Wyatt didn't care much for circumstances such as that himself. In fact it was those types of predicaments that prompted him to enact his own brand of justice. According to Bill Tilghman, "Wyatt believed that no man could follow the written law with efficiency or safety to himself. He was a man who could forget his badge, make his own law and rule, and enforce them in justice and fairness to all and defend himself at the same time, both physically and socially with the legal factions."[10]

Wyatt demonstrated his ability to enforce his own rules shortly after he was appointed assistant city marshal of Dodge in 1876. Late one evening, a prominent local politician ordered Wyatt to perform an official act that didn't look exactly right to him.[11] He refused to follow orders and challenged his superior's morals. Incensed by his disobedience, the politician attempted to rip the badge from Wyatt's vest where he had it pinned. Wyatt punched the man in the face as soon as he touched his shield and the man collapsed in a heap at the lawman's feet. A few more blows to the head rendered the man unconscious, and Wyatt then dragged the office holder's limp form to jail.

Treating the politician the same way any other member of the public would be treated for challenging an officer of the law and for disturbing the peace, Wyatt locked the man in a cell. The politician's friends arrived in force once they learned he had been incarcerated and tried to bail him out. Wyatt denied their request and informed the anxious associates that they would have to wait until police court convened the following morning to make an appeal for his release. By mid-afternoon the following day the politician was out of jail. He never questioned Wyatt's authority again.

James ushered his horse through the soggy soil and brush toward a bit of an incline that overlooked the route to the Cimarron. He was hungry and fighting the urge to hunt some game to satisfy his empty belly when a jackrabbit jumped up ahead of him. The rabbit went a few rods and then set up on his hind legs, making an easy shot. James stopped his horse and stared at the rabbit, thinking. There wasn't any time to kill the animal and skin and cook it. He made a big movement for his gun, which spooked the rabbit, and it scampered off.

James checked the sky for the position of the sun and determined it was close to noon. He dismounted and massaged the body parts that were sore from the two days of riding he had done.

He removed a thick strip of jerky from his saddlebags and tore off a hunk with his teeth. After washing down the tough meat with a swig of water from his canteen, he rolled a cigarette and thumbed a match into quick life. He took a drag from the cigarette while positioning his horse between himself and the brisk wind. A hot ash fell into some brush and James watched it make a fiery ring. When the ring got about an inch wide, he jabbed his thumb down on it and killed it. Holding the burning cigarette in his teeth, he grabbed the reins of his horse, pulled himself onto the animal's back, and continued on his way to the river.

Bat snapped his pocket watch open and stared at the second hand sweeping around the face. It was two o'clock. The wait had been long and his nerves were in a knot. Settled on either side of him, but spaced fairly well apart, were the other members of the posse.[12] All three were keeping watch with Bat. With the exception of the heavy clouds scudding across the sky, nothing was moving beyond the place where they were holed up. Their carbine rifles ready for use, Bat, Charlie, and Bill scanned the brush, scattered rocks, and mounds from left to right. Wyatt surveyed the area with his binoculars. Occasionally the sun would peak out of the clouds and flash in his eyes. He shaded the lenses with one hand so there would be no flashing reflections that could betray their position.

He saw nothing. Not a single thing. Time dragged on.

When Bat looked at his watch again, it was almost four o'clock. He stared consistently ahead, his eyes narrowing as he studied the contours of the land, waiting. And then he saw something. Wyatt noted in his autobiography that, "Masterson, who had the eye of a hawk, observed a rider." The men watched the horse and passenger closely. "That's Kenedy," Bat told the men, "I know him by the way he rides." Wyatt looked through his binoculars and brought the rider who was pointing his horse straight at the posse into focus. "He's right," Wyatt assured Charlie and Bill.

James urged his horse into a slight gallop, and the animal lifted his tired but proud head as he moved. His widespread nostrils greedily gulped the chilly air. For the moment nothing seemed out of the ordinary to the fugitive. There wasn't a hint of hesitation in the ride. Texas was all James could see.

CHAPTER EIGHT

CAPTURED

And in the twilight their man came.

BILL TILGHMAN'S WIFE ZOE RECOUNTING
WHAT BILL TOLD HER ABOUT TAKING
JAMES KENEDY INTO CUSTODY, 1949

James squirmed uncomfortably in the saddle and slowed his horse from a fast trot to a walk. The renegade's attention was fixed on the countryside that unrolled before him. There were miles and miles of open range as far as he could see. The sky directly above was clear with fuzzy pinches of cottonlike clouds scattered here and there, but dark thunderheads were piling up a few miles out. He led his horse around the bones of a buffalo that had fallen some time prior to his passing through the area, and the horse balked and snorted. The mount was apprehensive about moving forward. James strained his eyes over the rugged trail but failed to see anything that warranted the horse's obstinate behavior. He poked the animal with his spurs, and the horse continued on.

Bat peered over the mound of earth he and the other posse members were positioned behind and watched the fugitive they'd been pursuing slowly draw nearer. "We'll stop him out here," Wyatt announced. "I don't think he'll make a fight. Most likely he'll run for it." "If he does . . . I'll drop him," Charlie promised. "Kelley wants Kenedy alive," Bill reminded the men.[1]

Charlie looked around for their horses and noted that the animals were scattered about the vicinity—too far away for the lawmen to reach without being seen. "Damn it," Bat spat under his breath realizing along with Wyatt and Bill the location of the mounts. "I'll attend to the man," Bat told his fellow riders after contemplating the distance a bullet would have to travel to hit James. "If he runs, shoot his horse," Bat ordered Wyatt.[2]

James rode on lost in thought. The closer he got to the acres of pastureland outlining the sod house, the more nervous his horse became. The animal raised his head and neighed. James surveyed the region and again saw nothing out of the ordinary. He kept going but stopped every few yards to make sure the way was clear. Seventy-five yards away from the posse's location, James brought his ride to a stop.[3] He could hear only the cold wind blowing over the withered grass.

He scrutinized the prairie for a third time and noticed four riderless horses milling about. Anxiety swelled to fear and he broke out in a cold, clammy sweat. A charged silence fell over the area as the outlaw and the posse held their positions like graven images, waiting for someone to make a move. James's face was bloodless and in one quick simultaneous motion, he removed his gun from its holster and swung his horse around.

Wyatt, Bat, Charlie, and Bill jumped up and leveled their weapons at James. "Halt," Bat shouted, cocking his weapon. James was defiant. He fired a shot at the same time that he dug his spurs into his mount's sides.[4] The animal launched into a hard gallop. "Halt," Wyatt warned the killer again. James refused. "Last chance, Kenedy," Wyatt warned. "Halt!" James raised his whip to strike his ride and urge the horse to go faster, but a bullet fired from Bat's .50-caliber rifle struck his left shoulder and he dropped the quirt.[5] Thoroughly spooked by the violent exchange, the horse hurried to escape the scene. The lawmen let loose a volley of shots. Wyatt took careful aim and fired at James's horse. Three bullets brought the animal down. James fell out of the saddle just as his mount received the fatal shot. The horse landed hard on top of him, crushing the arm that had just been wounded. Horse and rider lay motionless on the ground.

Guns still at the ready, the posse cautiously made its way to the injured outlaw. James was writhing in pain when the lawmen reached him. The racehorse was dead and James was unable to pull himself out from under the animal. When the police officers reached the fugitive, they spread out around him. Charlie retrieved the two .44-caliber revolvers that James had dropped when he fell. Bill inspected the man's wound while Bat and Wyatt looked on.[6] "Did I get that bastard Kelley?" James asked, his face working with insane rage. "No, but you killed someone else," Wyatt told him. "Dora Hand was asleep in Kelley's bed." James was stunned by the news. His eyes slowly filled with torment and deep regret. He glanced over at his bleeding shoulder and then looked up at the rifle in Bat's hand. "You damn son-of-a-bitch!" he said, his voice sick with anguish. "You ought to have made a better shot than you did." "Well," Bat replied with great contempt, "you damn murdering son-of-a-bitch, I did the best I could."[7]

Bat bent down to pry James from beneath the horse. Wyatt, Charlie, and Bill raised the animal on one side and

James attempted to wriggle out. Bat grabbed the criminal's wounded arm and jerked the man free. The bones in his arm crunched loudly and James winced in pain. "You sons-of-bitches!" he shouted. "I'll get even with you for this."

Ignoring his remarks, Bat and Wyatt clamped a hand on each of his arms and pulled him up on his feet. "Which one of you shot my damn horse?" James demanded. "I did," Wyatt confessed remorsefully. "I hated to do it . . . but only because it was a beauty."[8]

The lawmen led the outlaw back to the sod ranch house where they bound and set James's shattered arm in a make-shift splint.[9] Blood from the rifle ball lodged in his shoulder saturated his shirt. His capturers had no sympathy for him. James had no sympathy for himself. He was horrified that he had killed a woman and further distressed by whom it was. As Bat gruffly secured his prisoner on a pack mule the ranch owner had loaned the posse, James fought off an overwhelming wave of emotion. Unconsciously, a smothered groan escaped him. "Dora's dead," he muttered sadly.

The posse mounted their horses and guided the animals in the direction of the place where Dodge City had come into its riotous existence. The smell of mud from the river permeated the air, and James glanced out across the prairie at the dark line of cottonwood trees lining the waterway in the near distance. The notion of how close he came to getting away would have been amusing if not for the fact that Dora was gone.

At one time he would have waded through Hell for one of her smiles, and now he'd never see her face again. He thought back on how she looked at a performance he had attended at the Comique Theatre. The dark-haired beauty had serenaded a full house with a haunting love song called "Lorena." Her exquisite voice combined with the brilliant costume she wore and the painted sets behind her were intoxicating to James. In spite of the distractions from the noisy audience and his view being impaired by the fog of the blue tobacco smoke, he remembered that his gaze remained on the entertainer. "Forgive me, Dora," James sadly mumbled.[10] Wyatt overheard the plea and glared at the fugitive as they rode on. "How do you forgive the devil?" Wyatt asked James incredulously.

More than thirty riders from the King Ranch raced across the Texas terrain toward Corpus Christi. Mifflin Kenedy, a lean, middle-aged man with a stern no-nonsense expression, wearing a tailor-made suit and vest with a gun in a high waistband, rode out front. There was a coiled energy to the group. They looked, acted, and were in any and all ways formidable. Their dried mud–splattered clothes and horses gave them a ghostlike appearance in the twilight.

The riders who followed the posse out of Dodge had informed Mifflin of the trouble his son was in. He wasted no time recruiting competent ranch hands to help find James and bring him home. They drove their mounts hard to a crossroad, where Mifflin waved his hand. The riders didn't stop as they split off into two groups. One headed northwest, in the direction of Kansas, and Mifflin and the other group proceeded into Corpus Christi.

After arriving at the train depot, the cattle baron and his men loaded their horses onto a livestock car then boarded a passenger car. Mifflin stared out the window at the busy town of Corpus Christi. The train's engine belched a trail of smoke as it pulled away from the station. A conductor passed through the car collecting the tickets of all those traveling north. Mifflin produced a ticket from his jacket and held it up for the man to take. The train whistle blew, and the transport slowly made its departure. The King Ranch cowhands removed their hats, reclined in their seats, and drifted off to sleep. Mifflin kept his focus fixed on the scenery. His thoughts centered on his son and what he'd have to do this time to help him.

A lengthy procession of mourners followed behind the prairie schooner that carried Dora Hand's remains. Grief-stricken saloon girls, cowboys, businessmen, and politicians wept for the murdered entertainer.[11] Some of the women carried flowers; the men held their hats in their hands and walked with their heads lowered in respect. The Reverend O. W. Wright led the march along Front Street to the Prairie Grove Cemetery where Dora would to be laid to rest.[12] With the exception of a few women who wailed loudly as they followed after Dora's casket, the parade was reverent and thoughtful.

On reaching the graveyard, the sorrowful attendees surrounded the open pit into which Dora's casket would be lowered. Wright officiated at the ceremony. Before reflecting on her charming personality and kind heart, he quoted from the book of John. The verse was meant for anyone who thought Dora was unworthy of such a send-off. "He that is without sin among you let him first cast a stone at her," the reverend said.

The combination oration and eulogy was hailed by everyone in attendance. One of the more than two hundred men on horseback who was at Dora's funeral noted that "never before had such a sermon been heard in Dodge City." The October 9, 1878, edition of the *Dodge City Times* also paid tribute to the murdered woman. The article read, "The deceased came to Dodge this summer and was a vocalist in the Varieties and Comique shows. She was a prepossessing woman and her artful winning ways brought many admirers within her smiles and blandishments. If we mistake not, Dora Hand has an eventful history. She applied for a divorce from Theodore Hand. After a varied life the unexpected death messenger cuts her down in the full bloom of gayety and womanhood. She was the innocent victim."

People returned to their daily business at the conclusion of the solemn service. There was very little conversation as they filtered off in various directions. Mayor James Kelley, who was on the mend from the severe spell of sickness that forced him to seek help from a doctor at Fort Dodge, lingered at the gravesite.[13] He was weak and grief-stricken and struggled to find the strength to walk away from the spot where Dora was buried. As he watched the mourners depart, he noticed a few well-dressed men on horseback a couple of hundred yards away. He recognized them as associates of Mifflin and James Kenedy.[14] Their presence at the funeral infuriated the mayor. He stared at the ranchers with a fierce look and stealthily moved his hand closer to his holstered six-shooter. They glared back at the politician. Bad tempers and festering grievances threatened to come to a head. A wry smile spread across the face of one of the cattlemen, as though he knew something the mayor didn't.

He turned his horse away from the cemetery, and the other riders followed suit. Mayor Kelley watched them ride off and disappear into the town.

Streams of sunlight poured out of the holes in the thunder-clouds converging over Dodge City. The posse and their prisoner rode quietly in and out of the beams of light, past the sprawl of buildings on either side of the main thoroughfare. On October 6, 1878, townspeople and homesteaders conducting business at the various feed stores and shops stopped what they were doing to watch the posse parade down the street with their prey.[15] Disgusted, James looked around at the curious faces. It was evident by the way he sat his horse that he was in terrible pain. The temporary bandages and splint wrapped around his arm were soaked through with blood.

Bat led the way to the sheriff's office with James and the mule he was riding in tow. When the lawmen reached the jail, they dismounted, but the captured outlaw didn't make any attempt to get off his mount.[16] His injury was so severe he couldn't lift himself out of the saddle. Tired and frustrated, Bat jerked the man off the horse. James yelped in pain. "You should have killed me," he said to Bat with a groan. "Don't think I didn't consider it," the lawman snapped back.

Bill escorted the criminal into the jail, and the other lawmen followed closely behind. James was deposited into a cell where he collapsed onto a worn-out bunk, crying and clutching his arm. Wyatt locked him in, and Charlie sent William Duffy to get a doctor. Bat watched the deputy walk up the street by the Lone Star Saloon where a half a dozen cowboys stood watching the jail. Bat knew them as men who rode for the King Ranch. He stepped outside the sheriff's office and stared them down; his blue eyes burned with anger. The cowboys looked away from Bat just as Deputy Duffy returned with Dr. T. L. McCarty. The doctor hurried inside, but Bat and William remained out in front of the building. The ranch hands slowly dispersed and headed off in the direction of the Lone Star Saloon.

The intrepid posse's return to Dodge with James Kenedy was the topic of conversation at every saloon, barbershop, hotel, and livery stable in town. The focus of conversation centered on the so-called trap the lawmen set to apprehend James. Newspaper accounts about what transpired were at odds with the actual event. Reports indicated that the lawmen anticipated the fugitive's every move and lured him to the homestead near the ford, making it appear as though they were not in the vicinity. The October 12, 1878, edition of the *Dodge City Times* noted that the "officers were lying in wait at Meade City, their horses unsaddled and grazing on the plain, the party avoiding the appearance of a sheriff's posse in full feather, believing that they were in advance of the object of their search, but prepared to catch any stray straggler that exhibited signs of distress."

News about the lawmen's dramatic pursuit of James Kenedy spread throughout the state. According to Wyatt Earp's biographer Stuart Lake, the publicity prompted several people to travel to Dodge to "see the intrepid officers for themselves." Legend has it that among those people was the famous publisher and dime novelist, Ned Buntline. Buntline was reportedly so affected by the posse's bravery that he commissioned the Colt manufacturing company to make special guns for each one of them. The Buntline Special had a twelve-inch barrel and included a fitted walnut stock.

The posse's members did not allow themselves to be preoccupied with the attention James Kenedy's arrest brought them. They arrived back in Dodge after the ordeal, tired and saddle sore. They made themselves comfortable in the sheriff's office while Dr. McCarty examined James. Wyatt struck a match as he seated himself behind the desk. A lamp caught smokily and filled the room with yellow light. Bat, Charlie, and Bill found places to sit down and rest their fatigued frames.

Nerves that had been taut with strain, relaxed. No one spoke. With the exception of the whimpers of pain emanating from James's cell, all was uncharacteristically quiet.

CHAPTER NINE

THE GUNMAN'S TRIAL

The wounded prisoner, Kenedy, is getting along finely.

FORD COUNTY GLOBE,
OCTOBER 16, 1878

The intensely focused surgeon carefully probed the bloody crater in James Kenedy's arm searching for the bullet lodged deep inside his flesh. Dr. McCarty's patient was pale and sweating profusely. He was semiconscious and in torment. James glanced at his quivering arm as if it belonged to someone else. Dr. McCarty was unmoved by the man's pleading look to stop. In the six years he practiced medicine in Dodge City, he had tended to numerous gunshot wounds.[1] He was competent but cared little about making sufferers like James comfortable until after he'd finished operating.

The doctor reached inside a metal pan next to the table and removed a pair of blood-soaked forceps placed there alongside a number of other medieval looking instruments. James fidgeted, and Dr. McCarty motioned for Bill Tilghman to hold him still so he could continue working.

James looked up at the lawman . . . A coherent understanding of all that had occurred flashed across his face, and he closed his eyes as if to block out the thought.

With no warning Dr. McCarty plunged the forceps into the bullet hole and James howled in pain. The agonizing wail reverberated through the sheriff's office and out of the building, spilling onto the street. The sound assaulted Wyatt's ears. He had been standing in front of the jail monitoring the comings and goings of the cowhands converging on the Lone Star Saloon. He was anticipating trouble. Should any of the drovers in town working for the King Ranch consider coming to James's aid, the lawman was ready for them.

Wyatt had been in a similar situation with a Texas prisoner the year before. The wealthy owner of the livestock marked the sale of his herd with a drunken shooting spree on Front Street. The inebriated man took the celebration into a saloon where he bought the house a round of drinks and danced with the soiled doves who worked there. After a disagreement with a fiddle player over a tune, the cattleman began beating the musician. Bleeding from a gash in his head, the musician managed to make it out of the tavern, but the hot-headed Texan was fast on his heels.

Wyatt wasted no time disarming the cattleman and hauling him to jail. Prosperous business associates and politicians close to the Texan demanded the lawman release their friend, and a crowd gathered outside the marshal's office. Bob Wright, a member of the Kansas state legislature, led the group in protesting Wyatt's actions. "You'll let him go if you know what's good for you," Bob barked. Wyatt ignored the warning and locked the door of the cell into which he had tossed the cattleman. Bob grabbed the lawman's arm to wrench the key away from him. "If you don't let him out, Dodge will have a new marshal tomorrow," the politician snapped. Wyatt muscled Bob into the cell with his friend. "If

I had done anything else," Wyatt later told Mayor Kelley, "I'd have to leave town, because I'd have lost whatever edge I've got with these troublemakers."[2]

James's pitiful groans of discomfort continued. Curious passersby paused momentarily to listen, then hurried on their way gossiping about the killer's fate. Movement in a partially opened upstairs window at the Great Western Hotel, across the street from the jail, caught Wyatt's attention. He looked up to see a distraught Fannie Garrettson staring down at the building. Troubled by James's cries, she shut the window. Wyatt had had his fill of the scene as well, and after considering his next move, he walked down the street and disappeared into the night.

Charlie Bassett checked the time on his pocket watch against the clock hanging over his desk in the marshal's office. He rubbed his tired eyes and turned his attention to the ledger and legal papers sprawled in front of him. Bookwork wasn't the most desirable aspect of the position, but it went with the job, and Bassett was pleased to note that the posse had been successful. The constant cries of anguish emanating from James's cell reminded him that not every pursuit ended well, however.

On October 22, 1877, convicted murderer and thief George Wilson escaped from the Dodge City jail, and Charlie led a manhunt to apprehend the outlaw. According to the *Dodge City Times,* October 27 edition, Bassett "issued a $50 reward for Wilson's return." The article described the man as "5 feet 11 inches tall, dark hair, blue eyes, good looking, straight built, 22 years old, small mustache and goatee, has a scar from a pistol shot in his back, wore dark clothes, and a wide-brimmed, white hat." Charlie and his posse were not able to catch the criminal. Authorities in Arkansas arrested Wilson in the fall of 1895, and he was executed shortly thereafter.

In the meanwhile Bat Masterson sought relief from the hard ride in a card game at the Long Branch Saloon. The tavern was busy, and a musician was attempting to entertain the group by pounding out songs on an out-of-tune piano. Bat studied the deck and the five cards in his hand, but his eyes and ears were alert to his surroundings. His brother Jim and a deputy, William Duffy, sat at one side of the bar nursing a drink. At the opposite end were four cowboys who rode for the King Ranch. They wore grim expressions and spoke in gruff, hushed tones.

A couple of jovial locals wandered into the saloon and bellied up to the bar between the men. One of the locals caught Bat's eye in the giant mirror lining the wall behind the bar and smiled. "I bet you can hear Kenedy hollering all the way to Ellsworth," he said to the lawmen. The drovers from the King Ranch shot the man a harsh look that promptly went ignored by everyone except Bat. "If he wants to avoid hardship," Bat said coolly, "he shouldn't go around shooting innocent women." The Texans glared at Bat. Unaffected, he leaned back in his chair and continued with his game. The cowhands ordered another round of drinks. Any animosity they felt over Bat's comment was soon tempered by several glasses of beer.

A mass of grey clouds hovered over Dodge the morning after James Kenedy was brought back to town. They spit a handful of raindrops that made dark splotches in the earth the size of silver dollars. The stagecoach driver, a heavy-set man with a scruffy beard that started just below his eyes and continued to his neck, loaded the top of the waiting vehicle with several trunks and leather bags. Once the luggage was secure, he gave his pocket watch a quick look and snapped it shut impatiently. "Time to board," he bellowed to a few passengers waiting inside a mercantile. Two of the passengers hurried out of the store carrying a few items of food. With the driver's assistance they climbed aboard the stage and made themselves comfortable.

The driver again announced that the stage was boarding. Fannie Garrettson stood in the entryway of the store, clutching a cloth satchel in her hand and studying the vehicle. "Are you leaving, Miss?" the driver asked. "I'm afraid I must," she finally replied. After one last look at Front Street, Fannie stepped into the stage, and the driver closed the door. The driver scaled the canvas-and-iron transport and sat down in a suddenly overburdened seat. He collected the reins that led to a team of horses and urged them forward. Fannie sat quietly and stared out her window. She wanted nothing more than to be out of the unpredictable town and free of the memory of Dora's brutal death.[3]

Less than two weeks after James Kenedy was arrested, Judge R. C. Cook deemed the accused was well enough to stand trial. One at a time the posse members converged at the sheriff's office where the trial was set to take place.[4] Wyatt passed by the stockyards on his way to the sheriff's office and spotted the laborer he had spoken to soon after Dora had been shot. The laborer was one of a handful of witnesses who could testify against James, having seen him ride out of town on his racehorse around the time the singer was killed.[5]

A pair of burly cowboys who Wyatt recognized as men who rode for Mifflin Kenedy stood in front of the stockyard worker speaking to him in low, curt tones. Their words flicked unpleasantly, and although Wyatt could not hear their conversation, he could tell the situation was heated. The ranch hands' fists were doubled at their sides, and the laborer they were talking to was backed against one of the stalls in the livery, afraid to move. When the two cowhands noticed Wyatt watching them, their demeanor changed. They pretended to be engaged in a light-hearted exchange with the laborer. They patted him on the back and led him away from the lawman, laughing and joking.

When Wyatt arrived at the sheriff's office, Mifflin Kenedy was there and the proceedings soon began. The preliminary examination was held in the cell next to James's. A battery of attorneys was present to represent the outlaw. There was no gallery area and no room for spectators.[6]

James was tired and uncomfortable. His arm was heavily bandaged and held tightly in place by a sling fashioned around his neck. His movements were feeble and slow and caused him excruciating pain. Judge Cook was not a man to be swayed by sickness or injury. He relied on proper marshaling of facts. The plaintiff had the burden of supplying evidence to justify a conviction. Law enforcement testified to James Kenedy's suspicious behavior the night of Dora Hand's murder and recounted his confession when he was arrested. No other witnesses appeared at the hearing.[7]

Several hours after the trial began, Charlie, Bill, Bat, and Wyatt filtered out of the building onto a relatively quiet street. The general activity around Dodge City had slowed while the hearing was going on. Some of the townspeople were milling about the thoroughfare and shop entrances awaiting a verdict. The four lawmen were frowning, but they said nothing to the citizens eagerly hoping for news. The door to the sheriff's office opened and James Kenedy's lawyers escorted their wounded client outside.

The murmur of the men's voices and the thud of their boots on the plank sidewalk made a rippling current of sound along the block. The intrepid posse's members watched in disgust as James was led away from the jail. The look of displeasure the freed man saw on the police officers' faces pleased him. He smiled smugly as his attorneys helped him down the street toward the Dodge City Hotel. Judge Cook emerged from the office and watched James walk away. He exchanged a somber look with the lawmen then headed off in the opposite direction of that taken by James and his representatives.

Taken aback by the outcome of the hearing, the townspeople solemnly continued their daily business. The posse members remained where they were for a moment, uncertain about what to do next. "There wasn't anyone," Wyatt said bitterly, "to champion the cause of Dora, who was without money or influence."[8] Scowling, he strode away from the building. One by one the others left the site as well.

The October 29, 1878, edition of the *Dodge City Times* reported that James Kenedy was released due to "insufficient evidence." The article read: "Kenedy, the man who was arrested for the murder of Fannie Keenan [a.k.a. Dora Hand], was examined before Judge (R. G.) Cook, and acquitted . . . We do not know what the evidence was, or upon what ground he was acquitted.

"But he is free to go on his way rejoicing whenever he gets ready."

Many of the Dodge City residents were outraged by James Kenedy's release. There was speculation that some of Mifflin Kenedy's rich associates furnished his son with the capital necessary to retain his high-priced attorneys.[9] The general consensus was that when Mifflin got to Dodge, he would reward his loyal friends monetarily or with future political endorsements. One of the posse members was able to determine the exact reason behind what seemed so flagrantly to be a miscarriage of justice. The idea that money and position could influence the court appalled them and altered their views of police work. Wyatt admitted that the outcome of James Kenedy's hearing left him disillusioned with law enforcement.[10] He grew even more embittered when the city council cut the police force's salary less than a month after James was released.

Wyatt continued to do his job with the same efficiency and courage as always, but with less patience than he had at one time. His name slipped from the local newspapers as his faith in the work continued to diminish, but an altercation with three drunken men traveling from Leadville, Kansas, to Missouri did put Wyatt back on the front page. The lawman arrested the men and was transporting them to jail when one of them pulled a gun and attempted to shoot him.

According to the May 10, 1879, edition of the *Dodge City Times,* "While Assistant Marshal Earp was attempting to disarm [them] and [was] leading an unruly cuss off by the ear, another one of the party told his chum to 'throw lead,' and endeavored to resist the officer. Sheriff Bat Masterson soon happened on the scene and belabored the irate Missourian, using the broadside of his revolver over his head. The party was disarmed and placed in the cooler."

Eleven days later, Wyatt was asked to serve a court order on a Texas drover who refused to pay one of his hands for the work he had done. Accompanied by fellow officer Jim Masterson, Wyatt presented the writ to the cattleman and his six herders. At first they resisted the lawmen, but the officers stood up to the hostile men, and the debt was promptly paid.[11]

The two volatile, publicized events along with the outcome of James Kenedy's case, hastened Wyatt's departure from Dodge. "I'd had a belly full of lawing," he recalled later in his memoirs.

Rather than leave the profession at that time, Bat sought to change the system from within. He was interested in politics and attended Republican conventions as a Ford County delegate. He maintained his position as sheriff while waiting for his political career to take off.

According to the December 10, 1878, edition of the *Ford County Globe,* the personal disappointment he experienced as a result of James Kenedy being set free in October was followed by a professional setback in December. Four prisoners managed to escape from Bat's jail. Dodge City residents who didn't like the sheriff, as well as some Texas cowboys who held a grudge against him, suggested the jailbreak was allowed to happen because the inmates were Bat's friends. Bat denied the claim and immediately left town with his deputy to apprehend the fugitives. Two of the four men were eventually recaptured, their apprehension being reported in the *Ford County Globe,* March 18, 1879.

Ford County commissioners who disapproved of the stern way Bat dealt with unruly cowhands, a parade of guilty thieves and murderers who had been arrested and escaped justice, and eventually being voted out of office took its toll on his perception of law enforcement. Less than two years after Dora Hand was killed, Bat was making plans to relocate and pursue another career.

Charlie Bassett's first term as marshal of Dodge City had been filled with tragedy and disenchantment. It started in April 1878 with the murder of Ed Masterson and concluded a year after Dora's untimely demise. The efficiency of his administration was recognized by the Ford County district court in January 1879. As reported in the *Dodge City Times,* on January 11, the court noted that "the large criminal calendar suggests the 'probability' of an 'endeavor' on the part of the officers to do their duty.

"To an unprejudiced person somebody has been making things lively. Sheriff Bat Masterson, Under Sheriff and Marshal Bassett, and Deputies (William) Duffy, and (James) Masterson, have evidently earned the high praise accorded to them for their vigilance and prompt action in the arrest of offenders of the law."

Given the discouraging result in the case against James Kenedy, Charlie considered the praise disingenuous.

Nonetheless, he remained dedicated to police work until his resignation from office in October 1879.[12]

Bill reacted to the release of James Kenedy by poring over the more than fifty volumes of law books at the county prosecuting office. His concern over the letter of the law baffled many of his cohorts, but his knowledge of the state and federal mandates aided his appointment as city marshal. Rowdy cowhands and aspiring criminals who misinterpreted his respect for the law as weakness and challenged his authority learned quickly that Bill was fearless. He disarmed many trail-stained strangers who threatened to shoot him or anyone else who lived in Dodge.[13]

A slender column of sunshine came down from above and ended in a pool of light that filled the back of the wagon where James Kenedy was lying.

His father sat in front of the vehicle that was being driven by one of the hands from the King Ranch. A half a dozen other gun-toting cowboys from the Texas spread rode alongside the wagon keeping a careful eye out for anyone who might attack them. James was being transported to Fort Dodge to undergo an operation on his arm.[14] The fortified escort was in place to ward off any vigilante groups daring enough to try and grab the injured cargo.

The trail between the military camp and Dodge City was rugged. Every bump the wagon came in contact with caused James pain. He gently held his well-bandaged arm close to his body and desperately tried to keep it still. He stifled a groan as the wagon plodded in and out of ruts. Mifflin glanced back at his son's tortured face and nodded reassuringly.

Shortly after they arrived at the military hospital at Fort Dodge, James was readied for a long and difficult surgery on his severely wounded arm. Dr. Blencowe Eardley Fryer, a respected Civil War surgeon from Fort Leavenworth, Kansas, helped perform the operation. United States Army Surgeon William Scott Tremaine, who was stationed at Fort Dodge at the time, helped with the procedure. Both doctors were assisted by James's attending physician in Dodge City, Dr. T. L. McCarty.

An article in December 17, 1878, edition of the *Ford County Globe* reported on the outcome of the dangerous surgical operation. "The Doctors took from the left shoulder of Mr. Kenedy several shattered bones, one being nearly five inches in length. The doctors experienced considerable difficulty in stopping the blood but finally succeeded. Though considerably exhausted from the slight loss of blood as well as from the shock experienced, Mr. Kenedy showed remarkable fortitude and nerve and said afterwards that he would not die from the effects of the operation. Just how the case will result is hard to conjecture, but life is hanging on a very slender cord. But as he is receiving the best medical attention, we predict for him a speedy recovery."

The Kenedys returned to Corpus Christi as soon as James was able.

Dodge City was a town tailored to fit the needs of range hands and soldiers hungry for pleasure and eager to forget hardships. There was an abundance of businesses that supplied drink, women, and games to help them do just that. The topic of Dora Hand's untimely death was soon replaced with conversation about the best places at which to spend the money that burned the fingers of men eager to turn their passions loose after long aching months of toil and sweat and cold and suffering on the plains.

For awhile another criminal shifted law enforcements attention away from James Kenedy. Henry Bourne, also known as Dutch Henry, was a murderer, mail robber, and horse thief. The outlaw had made a name for himself in several states. In January 1879, as reported on January 25, by the *Dodge City Times,* he was arrested in Colorado and Bat Masterson had him extradited to Dodge City to stand trial for stealing horses. The trial lasted two days and in the end, Dutch was found not guilty. The jury sighted "insufficient evidence" as the reason for acquittal. For the members of the intrepid posse the acquittal was a jarring reminder of what happened to Dora Hand's accused murderer.

CHAPTER TEN

END OF THE TRAIL

I'd had a belly full of lawing.

WYATT EARP, 1927

A fresh mound of earth covered Dora Hand's grave and a sweet breeze danced around the crudely fashioned marker stuck in the dirt where she had been buried. Several bouquets of wilted flowers encircled the wooden tombstone. Although their blooms had faded somewhat, they represented the only color in the soap-weed–infested cemetery. For a short time after James Kenedy's acquittal in late October 1878, mourners returned to Dora's plot to deposit fresh flowers, remember the entertainer, and reflect on the shooting that took her life.

The news of what James had done and the posse that pursued him followed the cattleman to Texas, and he reveled in the notoriety. Youth often wobbles dangerously, then steadies to follow the straight-and-narrow path, but not in his case. The injuries he sustained during his capture had left him a cripple, and he was anxious to prove that the disability had not affected his gunplay.

He learned to use his left arm to draw his weapon. The *Caldwell Commercial News,* December 6, 1880, reported rumors that he killed several men with his quick hand during a brief stay in Colorado in November 1880.

By 1882 James had settled down and married the daughter of a wealthy landowner. He focused on the family business and worked closely with his father, earning the man's respect and confidence. Neighbors and acquaintances— quoted in the *Corpus Christi Caller,* January 4, 1885—considered James to be a "man of industry with good business qualifications and a trusted manager of Mifflin's large ranch and cattle business."

James Kenedy died on December 29, 1884, of tuberculosis, shortly after his son, George Mifflin, was born.

News of Kenedy's death was slow to reach Dodge City, but it was well received when it got there. Mayor Kelley was particularly pleased. He had taken the death of Dora Hand hard. His emotional attachment to her, combined with the fact that a bullet intended for him had killed her, had left him devastated. Like many Dodge City residents who had been fond of Dora, Mayor Kelley felt "the only punishment meted out to James had been the sickness he endured from being shot by the posse," or so the *Dodge City Journal* observed in retrospect, in its June 30, 1938, edition. After James was apprehended, Mayor Kelley expected the gunslinger to be found guilty of murdering the songstress and subsequently hanged. The mayor was disappointed with the judge's ruling to acquit.

Mayor Kelley served four terms in office, stepping down from the position in March 1881. He left the job after being accused by his business partner of allowing a customer to pass a counterfeit dollar to him. In spite of the embarrassing incident, residents viewed Kelley as an effective town leader. The *High Plains Journal,* in a piece published on January 11, 1951, summarized his accomplishments: He helped pass ordinances outlawing houses of ill repute, increased licenses for taverns to help provide services to the community, and organized a law enforcement team that eventually became known throughout the territory as the "toughest group of men in the west."

With the exception of his daughter Irene, there was no other significant woman in Mayor Kelley's life. He consorted with very few ladies in public after the loss of Dora and focused much of his attention on his purebred greyhound dogs. In November 1885 a fire burned one of Mayor Kelley's saloons to the ground. He rebuilt the saloon, but he never fully recovered financially and was eventually forced to sell all of his real estate holdings to sustain himself.[1] When his health began to fail in late 1910, he moved to the Soldier's Home at Fort Dodge.

James Kelley died on September 8, 1912, from tuberculosis. He was seventy-nine years old. Friends and neighbors present at his funeral, held at the Fort Dodge church, stated that Mayor Kelley was "a figure not soon to be forgotten," as noted in the *Dodge City Times,* on September 10.

Unlike Mayor Kelley, Charlie Bassett opted to leave Dodge City after James Kenedy's trial. The lawman resigned his position and moved to New Mexico, where he went to work for Adams Express Company. He was employed as a guard for the rail and stage line that transported packages and supplies for businesses and private citizens to St. Louis, Missouri. He made frequent trips back to Dodge to visit friends, and they urged him to stay and run for sheriff. He refused, choosing instead to pursue a mining venture in Montana and business opportunities in Colorado and Texas. Charlie eventually settled in Kansas City, Kansas, where he owned and operated a number of saloons, as noted in the September 8, 1881, edition of the *Dodge City Times*.

A loyal friend to many of the men and women he met while living in Dodge, he could always be counted on to return to help if they needed him. Such was the case with his friend Luke Short in 1883. The *Dodge City Times,* on May 3, 1883, reported that three of the four "intrepid posse" members had come to Dodge to help Luke with his fight against local politicians and owners of a competing bar who were threatening to shut down his saloon. Charlie, Wyatt, and Bat, along with several other prominent western gunfighters, were able to help Luke end the conflict peacefully. The Dodge City War, as the incident would later be known, demonstrated the influence the men still had in the town.

When things calmed down, Charlie was asked to reconsider being nominated for sheriff, but he again declined. The "peace commissioners" who fought the corrupt Ford County government alongside the former lawman in the Dodge City War represented a more certain justice than the courts furnished. It was a notion that had become all the more attractive to the former marshal since witnessing the disappointing result of James Kenedy's hearing.[2]

Charlie died of inflammatory rheumatism on January 5, 1896. According to the January 9, 1896, edition of the *Globe Republican* newspaper, "Bassett was a cool and fearless officer. He had some good traits of character, and was a peaceable man." He was forty-nine years old when he passed away.

When James Kenedy was set free, Bat Masterson's interest in politics grew. He was weary of seeing men who had been arrested for various crimes acquitted. The January 14, 1879, edition of the *Ford County Globe* echoed Bat's sentiments by noting that sentencing of convicts in the area "have been almost as rare as angel's visits in the past—few and far between." He campaigned for men he thought would be tough on offenders and "make the way of transgressors hard." While working for the Republican Party, he maintained his duties as sheriff of Dodge City.

Bat successfully tracked down and arrested mail robbers, horse thieves, and murderers. He transported criminals to the state prison in Leavenworth and escorted renegade Indians back to the reservations from which they had escaped.

In May 1879, Bat thwarted an attempt to kill Wyatt Earp and himself by a handful of riders passing through Dodge from Clay County, Missouri. The drifters had had too much to drink and were causing a scene when, according to the May 10 issue of the *Dodge City Times,* Sheriff Masterson and Assistant Marshal Wyatt Earp were called in to disarm them. The men effectively relieved the rowdies of their guns and hauled them off to jail.

Soon after they were apprehended, the men were released and they set about making plans to assassinate the sheriff. Bat was made aware of what was happening and eventually one of the riders was rearrested. The men remarked that they "had run things in Missouri" and believed they could "take" Dodge City. They admitted later that they were "no match for Dodge City officers."

In spite of the high opinion criminals had for the lawman and the confidence Ford County residents had in his ability to make necessary arrests, Bat lost his bid to be reelected sheriff in late 1879.

Less than a year after Dora Hand was killed, Kansas voters cast their ballots for George Hinkel. On October 28, the *Ford County Globe* reported that Hinkel's more civilized approach to the job promised to save taxpayers the expense of pursuing alleged lawbreakers who would later be found not guilty. Bat was unhappy with the outcome and according to the November 8, 1879, edition of the *Speareville News,* he reportedly claimed that he was "going to whip every son-of-a-bitch that worked and voted against him in the county."

Bat left office in February 1880 and made his way to the Colorado gold fields. Like Charlie Bassett, he made several trips back to Dodge City from other locales such as Ogalala, Nebraska, Kansas City, Kansas, and Tombstone, Arizona. His visits usually coincided with a friend or relative being in trouble and needing his assistance. One such request for help came in April 1881 and resulted in a shootout between saloon owner A. J. Peacock, his bartender Al Updegraff, and

Bat Masterson. Bat shot Updegraff in the chest and was later arrested for disturbing the peace.

Bat's skill with a six-shooter and his reputation as a tough law enforcement officer who had helped recruit the most "intrepid posse" in the Old West made him a legend throughout the wild frontier. He used his notoriety to campaign for various politicians running for office in Dodge City and secure his own byline on a series of articles for the *Ford County Globe* newspaper. The *Dodge City Times* recognized his talent and praised him as a newspaper writer. "Col. Bat Masterson, a well-known character in the west," a November 1, 1883, article read, "has discarded his former illegitimate business and has adopted newspaper writing as a profession. While Col. Masterson's literary effusions do not have moral or religious tendencies, they are chaste productions in a literary way. The fine artistic style in which Col. Masterson wields the pen is adding fame to his already illustrious name."

From 1883 to 1890, Bat drifted about the West earning his income gambling, writing articles for various newspapers, and investing in theatrical productions, racehorses, and prizefighters. On November 21, 1891, he married Emma Walters and the pair lived in Coronado County, Kansas, and Creede, Colorado. Bat laid down his guns before settling in New York, where he was employed as a sports writer for the *New York Morning Telegraph*.

Ten years after Emma and Bat wed, President Theodore Roosevelt offered him the position as United States Marshal of Oklahoma. Bat declined the appointment and told the president that he wasn't the right man for the job. "Oklahoma is still woolly," Bat said, "and if I were marshal, some youngster would want to try and put me out because of my reputation.

"I have taken my guns off and I don't ever want to put them on again."[3]

The *Kansas City Daily Drover Telegram* of November 4, 1921, noted that Bat Masterson died quietly at his desk in New York on October 25. He had been suffering from a severe cold several days prior to his death. His heart stopped while he was working on an article about a boxer named Lew Tendler. His body was found clutching a pen in the hand he once used to shoot James Kenedy.

Wyatt Earp rode out of Dodge City in September 1879 after resigning from the police force he'd been a part of for more than three years. His interest in law enforcement shifted to gambling and mining, and after a brief stay in Las Vegas, New Mexico, he moved on to Tombstone, Arizona. He bought and sold various mining claims in the area, making a small fortune in the process. The November 27, 1880, edition of the *Dodge City Times* reported on Wyatt's windfall. It also included an article from a Texas newspaper, the *Caldwell Commercial,* that mistakenly declared his death at the hand of James Kenedy. The article stated that Wyatt was "shot and killed on Sand Creek, Colorado by James Kenedy of Texas . . . Earp shot and wounded Kenedy in the shoulder a year or two before, and meeting at Sand Creek both pulled their revolvers, but Kenedy got his work in first, killing Earp instantly. The above statement is not believed in Dodge City."

The statement was not believed in Tombstone either, where Wyatt had purchased an interest in the Oriental Saloon and was working as a dealer and peacekeeper. By late 1881 Wyatt Earp and his brothers were reported to be three of the wealthiest men in Cochise County, Arizona, in the October 11 issue of the *Ford County Globe*.

A feud between the Earps and a group of cattle and horse thieves known as the Cowboys eventually took Wyatt's attention away from his business pursuits. Wyatt's older brother Virgil accepted a job as marshal of Tombstone and deputized Wyatt and their younger brother Morgan to help him keep the Cowboys under control. On October 25, 1881, Virgil arrested Ike Clanton, a prominent member of the Cowboys, for drunk and disorderly conduct. The justifiable jailing sparked the famous gunfight that occurred the following day, and was recounted in the *Ford County Globe* on November 8.

The shootout near the OK Corral left three men—Billy Clanton, Frank McLaury, and Tom McLaury—dead. A few months later the Cowboys retaliated. They shot and permanently disabled Virgil and killed Morgan by shooting him in the back. Convinced the law would never prosecute the gunmen who had ambushed his family, Wyatt organized a posse to deal with the guilty parties themselves. In due time all 150 Cowboys were tracked down and killed.[4]

Wyatt's actions were controversial, but given the fact that he'd seen more than one murderer go free, he felt his behavior was moral and reasonable.

Wyatt returned to Dodge City twice in 1883 and both times it was to support friends in need. Nothing he did outside of the time spent in Tombstone and Dodge ever came close to achieving the fame he gained at those historic locations. He married actress Josephine Marcus in San Francisco, California, and chased rumors of gold to Shoshone, Idaho, and Nome, Alaska. He was a prospector in Goldfield, Nevada, and owned and operated a saloon in nearby Tonopah. He worked as a private detective on the Mexican border and raised thoroughbred horses in San Diego.

In 1897 President William McKinley offered Wyatt the job of United States Marshal for Arizona, but he turned the job down. He settled in the Southern California area in 1905, where he divided his time between his mining properties and oil wells in Oakland and Los Angeles.

"I'm not ashamed of anything I ever did," Wyatt said in 1927. "Were it to be done over again, I would do exactly as I did at the time. If the outlaws and their friends and allies imagined that they could intimidate or exterminate the Earps by a process of assassination, and then hide behind alibis and the technicalities of the law, they simply missed their guess."[5]

Wyatt Earp died on January 13, 1929, at his home in Los Angeles. He was eighty years old.

A profound silence reigned over the cemetery where Bill Tilghman stood next to Dora Hand's grave. Several months had past since the posse had returned with James Kenedy in tow. Bill shaded his tawny, mustached face from the sun and looked at the street spread out before him with the careful eye of one who had spent many years of his life analyzing and predicting the vagaries of rowdy cowhands and restless pioneers. He would spend the next eleven years keeping the peace in Ford County.

As city marshal he was credited with bringing in several outlaws and horse and mule thieves. Dodge City residents admired Bill's respect for the law and had the utmost confidence in his law enforcement talents. Their appreciation was made evident in an article that appeared in the November 11, 1884, edition of the *Ford County Globe*. "We feel proud of the fact that there was no need of a large extra police force in this city on election day," the piece read. "Marshal Tilghman and his usual daily force attended to their duties nobly and peace and quiet was the order of the day."

In 1889 the government opened up the Indian territory in the western half of Oklahoma, and Bill decided to leave Dodge in favor of securing ranch land for a cattle business. He was one of the first people to settle in the town of Guthrie. After being named United States Deputy Marshal of Oklahoma, Bill acted quickly to stamp out the outlawry that was rearing its head in newly established Lincoln County. He remained the territorial marshal for more than two decades, apprehending and arresting such well-known criminals as Bill Raidler, Kid Donner, John Braya, and Bill Doolin, and earning a reputation for never killing unnecessarily. Bat Masterson wrote, "It would take a volume the size of an encyclopedia to record the many daring exploits and adventures of this remarkable man."[6]

Bill retired from law enforcement in 1910 and became a state senator. In addition to politics, he pursued a career in filmmaking. He wrote, directed, and starred in a movie entitled *The Passing of the Oklahoma Outlaws*. In 1923, at the age of seventy, he came out of retirement and took a police job in Cromwell, Oklahoma. He was murdered on November 1, 1924, by a corrupt prohibition agent named Wiley Lynn. Lynn, like James Kenedy, was acquitted after several of the witnesses to the shooting, allegedly intimidated, failed to appear.

NOTES

Chapter One: Murder of a Nightingale

1   *Ford County Globe,* October 8, 1878; Vestal, *Queen of Cowtowns,* 162; Lowther, *Dodge City, Kansas,* 106.
2   Wesley, "Dora Hand," 14; Forrest, "Dora Hand," 48.
3   New England Historical Genealogical Research Report, March 26, 2007.
4   *Ford County Globe,* December 17, 1878; Streeter, *Prima Donna,* 30.
5   *St. Louis Daily Journal,* October 11, 1878; Wesley, "Dora Hand," 14; Forrest, "Dora Hand," 48.
6   *St. Louis Daily Journal,* October 11, 1878; Young, *Dodge City,* 106.
7   Lowther, *Dodge City, Kansas,* 177.
8   *Ford County Globe*, October 8, 1878; Vestal, *Queen of Cowtowns*, 162; Lowther, *Dodge City, Kansas*, 106.
9   Petition, Dora Hand vs. Theodore Hand, prepared by Harry E. Gryden, September 1878; *Dodge City Journal,* June 30, 1938.
10   Lowther, *Dodge City, Kansas,* 180.
11   DeArment, *Bat Masterson*, 118; Nash, *Encyclopedia of Western Lawmen & Outlaws*, 198.
12   Parsons, *James W. Kenedy*, 9; Hoyt, *Frontier Doctor,* 56.
13   Lowther, *Dodge City, Kansas,* 180.
14   Fannie Garrettson letter to Messrs. Eshers dated October 5, 1878.

Chapter Two: Cold-Blooded Assassin

1   Vestal, *Queen of Cowtowns,* 162; Young, *Dodge City,* 106.
2   Fannie Garrettson, letter to Messrs. Eshers, October 5, 1878.
3   Ibid.
4   DeArment, *Bat Masterson,* 120.
5   Parsons, *James W. Kenedy,* 9; DeArment, *Bat Masterson,* 116; Carter, *Cowboy Capital of the World,* 124.
6   Lowther, *Dodge City, Kansas,* 177.
7   DeArment, *Bat Masterson,* 118.
8   Vestal, *Queen of Cowtowns,* 163.
9   *San Francisco Examiner,* August 16, 1896; Tefertiller, *Wyatt Earp,* 28.
10 Tilghman, *Marshal of the Last Frontier,* 139; Miller, *Bill Tilghman,* 173.
11 Wesley, "Dora Hand," 14.
12 Lowther, *Dodge City, Kansas,* 181.
13 Vestal, *Queen of Cowtowns,* 164.
14 DeArment, *Bat Masterson,* 118; *Dodge City Times,* October 12, 1878.
15 Wright, *Dodge City,* 174.
16 Nolan, *Tascosa,* 54.
17 Lowther, *Dodge City, Kansas,* 182.
18 Miller and Snell, *Great Gunfighters,* 232.
19 Fannie Garrettson, letter to Messrs. Eshers, October 5, 1878.

Chapter Three: A Posse on the Move

1   *Kansas Historical Quarterly,* April 1960.
2   Tilghman, *Marshal of the Last Frontier,* 130; Jahns, *Doc Holliday,* 101.

3   Miller and Snell, *Great Gunfighters,* 27–30.

4   DeMattos, "The Dodge Citians," 113.

5   Miller and Snell, *Great Gunfighters,* 31.

6   Vestal, *Queen of Cowtowns,* 103.

7   Parsons, *James W. Kenedy,* 5–7.

8   Chrisman, *Ladder of Rivers,* 117–123.

9   Parsons, *James W. Kenedy,* 7.

10   DeArment, *Bat Masterson,* 122; Lowther, *Dodge City, Kansas,* 182.

11   Vestal, *Queen of Cowtowns,* 164.

Chapter Four: Thunder Over the Prairie

1   Hoyt, *Frontier Doctor,* 446; Nolan, *Tascosa,* 52–53.

2   Ohnick, "The Jones and Plummer Trail"; Vestal, *Queen of Cowtowns,* 164.

3   Vestal, *Queen of Cowtowns,* 165.

4   Carter, *Cowboy Capital of the World,* 124.

5   Tilghman, *Marshal of the Last Frontier,* 141; Lake, *Wyatt Earp*, 218. Stuart Lake's book was used as a point of reference four times in this manuscript. Since 1964 many historians have criticized Lake's work and attempted to debunk the material. Loren D. Estleman, an author who specializes in the historical western genre, said Lake's book "has been scorned repeatedly by historians of the revisionist type, who in their fanatical pursuit of Truth often gallop straight past the facts." Although it can be argued that Lake's position was definitely in favor of his subject, Wyatt Earp, continued research now indicates that Lake was more accurate than critics initially gave him credit for.

6   Haley, interview with Johnson.

7   Tilghman, *Marshal of the Last Frontier,* 13.

8   Vestal, *Queen of Cowtowns,* 97.

9   Tilghman, *Marshal of the Last Frontier,* 14.

10 Tefertiller, *Wyatt Earp,* 28.

Chapter Five: Caught in a Storm

1   Miller, *Bill Tilghman,* 52.

2   Carter, *Cowboy Capital of the World,* 191.

3   Tefertiller, *Wyatt Earp,* 5; DeArment, *Bat Masterson,* 19.

4   DeArment, *Bat Masterson,* 63.

5   Roberts, "Bat Masterson and the Sweetwater Shootout," 18.

6   Miller and Snell, *Great Gunfighters,* 193.

7   DeArment, *Bat Masterson,* 10.

8   O'Connor, *Young Bat Masterson,* 28.

9   DeArment, *Bat Masterson,* 32.

10 *Leavenworth Daily Commercial,* July 26, 1874.

11 O'Connor, *Young Bat Masterson,* 29.

12 *Dodge City Times,* June 6, 1877; Miller and Snell, *Great Gunfighters,* 202–203.

13 *Dodge City Times,* October 13, 1877; O'Connor, *Young Bat Masterson,* 77.

14 *Dodge City Times,* April 13, 1878; DeArment, *Bat Masterson,* 35.

15 Leavitt, *1878 Farmer's Almanack,* 25; Vestal, *Queen of Cowtowns,* 165.

Chapter Six: Beyond the River

1   O'Connor, *Young Bat Masterson,* 32.

2   Masterson, *Famous Gunfighters,* 54.

3   Barra, *Inventing Wyatt Earp,* 22.

4   Masterson, *Famous Gunfighters,* 55.

5   Nash, *Encyclopedia of Western Lawmen & Outlaws,* 301; Lake, *Wyatt Earp,* 91–92; Tefertiller, *Wyatt Earp,* 8.

6   Barra, *Inventing Wyatt Earp,* 26–27.

7   Masterson, *Famous Gunfighters,* 56

8   Tilghman, *Marshal of the Last Frontier,* 147.

9   Lake, "Straight Shooting Dodge," n.p.; Vestal, *Queen of Cowtowns,* 100.

10   *Dodge City Times,* July 26, 1877; Miller and Snell, *Great Gunfighters,* 87.

11   Tefertiller, *Wyatt, Earp,* 29.

Chapter Seven: Waiting for a Killer

1   Leavitt, *1878 Farmer's Almanack,* 25.

2   Nolan, *Tascosa,* 52.

3   Parsons, *James W. Kenedy,* 7.

4   DeArment, *Bat Masterson,* 94.

5   Miller, *Bill Tilghman,* 83.

6   Tilghman, *Marshal of the Last Frontier,* 143.

7   Vestal, *Queen of Cowtowns,* 164.

8   Miller and Snell, *Great Gunfighters,* 25.

9   Charlie Bassett, Letter to Gov. Thomas A. Osborn, April 28, 1976.

10   Tilghman, *Marshal of the Last Frontier,* 82.

11   Masterson, *Famous Gunfighters,* 57.

12   DeArment, *Bat Masterson,* 123.

Chapter Eight: Captured

1   *Dodge City Times,* October 12, 1878; Wright, *Dodge City,* 174.
2   Tefertiller, *Wyatt Earp,* 29.
3   Wright, *Dodge City,* 175.
4   Tilghman, *Marshal of the Last Frontier,* 142; Parsons, *James W. Kenedy,* 10.
5   DeArment, *Bat Masterson,* 123.
6   Vestal, *Queen of Cowtowns,* 6.
7   Barra, *Inventing Wyatt Earp,* 86; Lake, *Wyatt Earp,* 217–219.
8   Lake, *Wyatt Earp,* 86, 217–219.
9   Wright, *Dodge City,* 175; DeArment, *Bat Masterson,* 123.
10   Carter, *Cowboy Capital of the World,* 126.
11   Forrest, "Dora Hand," 52.
12   Sherer, *Pioneer History & Stories,* 45.
13   DeArment, *Bat Masterson,* 118.
14   Wesley, "Dora Hand," 13–14.
15   Miller and Snell, *Great Gunfighters,* 235.
16   Ibid.

Chapter Nine: The Gunman's Trial

1   Time Life Editorial Staff, *Townsmen,* 23.
2   Lake, *Wyatt Earp,* 173–174; Vestal, *Queen of Cowtowns,* 101–102.
3   Young, *Dodge City,* 107.
4   Miller and Snell, *Great Gunfighters,* 235.
5   Lowther, *Dodge City, Kansas,* 182.
6   Tefertiller, *Wyatt Earp,* 29.

7   Barra, *Inventing Wyatt Earp,* 86.
8   Ibid.
9   Carter, *Cowboy Capital of the World,* 126.
10 Barra, *Inventing Wyatt Earp,* 86.
11 *Dodge City Times,* May 24, 1879; Miller and Snell, *Great Gunfighters,* 263.
12 Miller and Snell, *Great Gunfighters,* 31.
13 Miller, *Bill Tilghman,* 82; Masterson, *Famous Gunfighters,* 52–53; Nash, *Encyclopedia of Western Lawmen & Outlaws,* 303.
14 Nolan, *Tascosa,* 57.

Chapter Ten: End of the Trail

1   Ary, "James 'Dog' Kelley," n.p.
2   Masterson, *Famous Gunfighters,* 29; Haywood, *Cowtown Lawyers,* 82.
3   Alexander, *Legends of the Old West,* 48.
4   E.B. Colburn, Letter to *Ford County Globe,* May 23, 1882.
5   Lake, *Wyatt Earp,* 377.
6   Masterson, *Famous Gunfighters,* 52.

Bibliography

Alexander, Kent. *Legends of the Old West.* New York: Michael Friedman Publishing Group, 1994.

Ary, Neal, "James 'Dog' Kelley A Part of the Legend." Independent paper written for Kansas Heritage Center, May 12, 1994.

Barra, Allen. *Inventing Wyatt Earp: His Life and Many Legends.* New York: Carroll & Graf Publishers, 1998.

Bassett, Charlie. Letter to Gov. Thomas A. Osborn, April 28, 1976.

Beebe, Lucius, and Charles Clegg. *The American West: The Pictorial Epic of a Continent.* New York: E. P. Dutton & Company, 1955.

Braddock, Betty, and Jeanie Covalt. *Dodge City.* Dodge City: Kansas Heritage Center, 1982.

Carter, Samuel III. *Cowboy Capital of the World: The Saga of Dodge City.* Garden City, N.Y.: Doubleday & Company, 1973.

Chrisman, Harry E. *The Ladder of Rivers: The Story I. P. (Print) Olive.* Athens: Swallow Press Books/Ohio University Press, 1965.

Crutchfield, James A., Bill O'Neal, and Dale L. Walker. *Legends of the Wild West.* Lincolnwood, Ill.: Publications International, 1995.

DeArment, Robert K. *Bat Masterson: The Man and the Legend.* Norman: University of Oklahoma Press, 1979.

DeMattos, Jack, "The Dodge Citians: Charles E. Bassett." *The Quarterly of the National Association for Outlaw and Lawman History, Inc.,* 19, no. 4 (October–December 1995).

Forrest, Earle. "Dora Hand: The Dance Hall Singer of Old Dodge City." *Los Angeles Corral Newsletter*, no. 7 (1957).

Foy, Eddie, and Alvin C. Harlow. *Clowning Through Life.* New York: E. P. Dutton and Company, 1928.

Haley, J. Evetts "White," interview with J. Arthur Johnson, March 27, 1946, Midland, Texas. Item available at the California History Room, Sacramento, Calif.; Hoyt, 92.

Haywood, Robert C. *Cowtown Lawyers: Dodge City and Its Attorneys.* Norman: University of Oklahoma Press, 1988.

Hoyt, Henry F. *A Frontier Doctor.* Boston: Houghton Mifflin Company, 1929.

Jahns, Pat. *The Frontier World of Doc Holliday.* New York: Indian Head Books, 1957.

Jenkner, Carol. "A Legendary Life in the Southwest." *Kansas Newsletter,* Spring 2005.

Kansas Historical Quarterly, November 1935, no. 4.

Kansas Historical Quarterly 22, no. 4 (Winter 1956).

Kansas Historical Quarterly 26 (April 1960).

Kansas Historical Quarterly 28, no. 3 (Autumn 1962).

Lake, Stuart N. "Straight Shooting Dodge." *Saturday Evening Post,* March 8, 1930.

———. *Wyatt Earp: Frontier Marshal.* New York: Pocket Books, 1931.

Leavitt, William, *1878 Farmer's Almanack*, LXXXII: 25.

Lowther, Charles C. *Dodge City, Kansas.* Philadelphia, Penn.: Dorrance & Company, 1940.

Masterson, W. B. (Bat). *Famous Gunfighters of the Western Frontier.* Houston: Frontier Press of Texas, 1907.

Miller, Floyd. *Bill Tilghman: Marshal of the Last Frontier.* Garden City, N.Y.: Doubleday & Company, 1968.

Miller, Nyle, and Joseph Snell. *Great Gunfighters of the Kansas Cowtowns.* Lincoln: University of Nebraska Press, 1963.

Nash, Jay Robert. *Encyclopedia of Western Lawmen & Outlaws.* New York: Paragon House, 1989.

New England Historical Genealogical Research Report, March 26, 2007.

Nolan, Frederick. *Tascosa: Its Life and Gaudy Times.* Lubbock: Texas Tech University Press, 2007.

O'Connor, Richard. *Young Bat Masterson.* New York: McGraw-Hill Book Company, 1967.

Ohnick, Nancy. "The Jones and Plummer Trail." www.vlib .us/old_west/trails/jonesplummer.html.

Parsons, Chuck. *James W. Kenedy: Fiend in Human Form.* Galway, Ireland: Western Publications Limited, 2001.

Peterson, Harold. *The Remington Historical Treasury of American Guns.* New York: Grosset & Dunlap, 1922.

Petition, Dora Hand vs. Theodore Hand, prepared by Harry E. Gryden, September 1878.

Reader's Digest Editorial Staff. *Legendary Characters of the Old West.* Pleasantville, N.Y.: Reader's Digest Association, 1976.

Roberts, Gary L. "Bat Masterson and the Sweetwater Shootout." *Wild West Magazine,* October 2000: 18.

Sherer, Jim. *Pioneer History & Stories: Dodge City & Ford County, Kansas, 1870–1920.* Dodge City: Kansas Heritage Center, 1996.

Snell, Joseph. "Painted Ladies of the Cowtown Frontier." *The Westerners Trail Guide* X, no. 4 (December 1965).

Streeter, F. B., "Prima Donna of Dodge City." *Kansas Historical Quarterly* 4, no. 4 (November 1935): 30.

Tefertiller, Casey. *Wyatt Earp: The Life Behind the Legend.* New York: John Wiley & Sons, 1997.

Tilghman, Zoe. *Marshal of the Last Frontier: Life and Services of William Matthew (Bill) Tilghman.* Glendale, Calif.: Arthur H. Clark Company, 1949.

————. *Outlaw Days.* Oklahoma City, Okla: Harlow Publishing Company, 1926.

Time Life Editorial Staff. *The Townsmen.* Alexandria, Va.: Time Life Books, 1975.

Vestal, Stanley. *Queen of Cowtowns: Killing of Dora Hand.* New York: Harper & Brothers, 1952.

Wesley, Ray, "Dora Hand," *Fur, Fish & Game Magazine,* November–December 1927: 14.

Wright, Robert. *Dodge City: The Cowboy Capital & the Great Southwest.* Wichita, Kans.: Wichita Eagle Press, 1913.

Young, Frederic R. *Dodge City: Up Through a Century in Story and Pictures.* Dodge City, Kans.: Boot Hill Museum, 1972.

Zauner, Phyllis. *Those Legendary Men of the Old West.* Sonoma, Calif.: Zanel Publications, 1998.

Newspapers

Caldwell Commercial News. December 6, 1880.

Corpus Christi Caller. January 4, 1885.

Dodge City Times.

March 31, 1877.	October 27, 1877.
June 6, 1877.	February 9, 1878.
July 21, 1877.	April 13, 1878.
July 26, 1877.	May 1878.
October 13, 1877.	August 10, 1878.

October 5, 1878.

October 9, 1878.

October 12, 1878.

October 29, 1878.

January 11, 1879.

January 25, 1879.

May 10, 1879.

May 24, 1879.

November 27, 1880.

September 8, 1881.

May 3, 1883.

November 1, 1883.

September 10, 1912.

Dodge City Journal. June 30, 1938.

Ellsworth Reporter. August 1, 1872.

Ford County Globe.

May 14, 1877.

July 30, 1878.

February 5, 1878.

April 23, 1878.

August 27, 1878.

September 24, 1878.

October 8, 1878.

October 16, 1878.

December 10, 1878.

December 17, 1878.

January 14, 1879.

March 18, 1879.

April 15, 1879.

September 9, 1879.

October 28, 1879.

October 11, 1881.

October 19, 1881.

November 8, 1881.

November 11, 1884.

Globe Republican. January 9, 1896.

High Plains Journal. January 11, 1951.

Kansas City Daily Drover Telegram. November 4, 1921.

Leavenworth Daily Commercial, July 26, 1874.

St. Louis Daily Journal. October 11, 1878.

San Francisco Examiner. August 16, 1896.

Spearville News. November 8, 1879.

INDEX

About the Authors

Howard Kazanjian is an award-winning producer and entertainment executive who has been producing feature films and television programs for more than twenty-five years. While vice president of production for Lucasfilm Ltd., he produced two of the highest grossing films of all time: *Raiders of the Lost Ark* and *Star Wars: Return of the Jedi*. He also managed the production of another top-ten box office hit, *The Empire Strikes Back*. Some of his other notable credits include *The Rookies, Demolition Man,* and the two-hour pilot and first season of *JAG*.

In addition to his production experience, Kazanjian has worked with some of the finest directors in the history of cinema. He has worked closely with such legends as Alfred Hitchcock, Billy Wilder, Sam Peckinpah, Robert Wise, Joshua Logan, Clint Eastwood, George Lucas, Steven Spielberg, and Francis Ford Coppola. He is a longtime voting member of the Academy of Motion Picture Arts and Sciences, the Academy of Television Arts and Sciences, the Producers Guild of America, and the Directors Guild of America. The California native is also a trustee of Azusa Pacific University.

Chris Enss is an award-winning screenwriter who has written for television, short subject films, live performances, and for the movies, and is the coauthor (with JoAnn Chartier) of *Love Untamed: True Romances Stories of the Old West, Gilded Girls: Women Entertainers of the Old West,* and *She Wore a Yellow Ribbon: Women Patriots and Soldiers of the Old West,* as well as *The Cowboy and the Senorita* and *Happy Trails* (with Howard Kazanjian). Her most recent books include *Frontier Teachers: Stories of Heroic Women of the Old West* and *A Beautiful Mine: Women Prospectors of the Old West.*

Enss has done everything from stand-up comedy to working as a stunt person at the Old Tucson Movie Studio. She learned the basics of writing for film and television at the University of Arizona, and she is currently working with Howard Kazanjian on the movie version of *The Cowboy and the Senorita,* their biography of western stars Roy Rogers and Dale Evans.